REAL ESTATE NOTE INVESTING

REAL ESTATE
NOTE
INVESTING

Using Mortgage Notes to Passively
and Massively Increase Your Income

DAVE VAN HORN

BiggerPockets®
PUBLISHING

Real Estate Note Investing
Dave Van Horn

Published by BiggerPockets Publishing LLC, Denver, CO
Copyright © 2018 by Dave Van Horn
All Rights Reserved.

Publisher's Cataloging-in-Publication data

Names: Van Horn, Dave, author.

Title: Real estate note investing : using mortgage notes to passively and massively increase your income / by Dave Van Horn.

Description: Includes bibliographical references. | Denver, CO: BiggerPockets Publishing, 2018.

Identifiers: ISBN 978-0-997584-77-6 | LCCN 2017960651

Subjects: LCSH Real estate investing. | Mortgages--United States. | Discounted mortgages--United States. | Finance, personal. | Real property--Purchasing--United States. | House buying--United States. | House selling--United States. | Mortgage loans--United States. | Wealth. | BISAC BUSINESS & ECONOMICS / Real Estate / Mortgages

Classification: LCC HD255 .V36 2018 | DDC 332.6/324--dc23

Published in the United States of America

10 9 8 7 6 5 4 3 2 1

Table of Contents

INTRODUCTION
The Accidental Note Investor

Real estate networking meetings tend to all look the same. They're held in either a ballroom in a local Holiday Inn or a small banquet hall in a decent restaurant. Both *banquet hall* and *ballroom* sound much too elegant for what's really going on in these places—a meeting of minds. It's basically just a room full of, more or less, middle-class men and women aged twenty-five to sixty (with some exceptions, of course) all looking to get ahead. I didn't know any of this going into my first meeting, of course, but it's something I've come to notice over the years.

Looking back now, I realize I didn't know what I was getting myself into the first time I walked into that ballroom full of real estate investors. As a newer real estate investor myself, I had already achieved my personal BHAG (big hairy audacious goal), which was to buy my first property. In fact, before attending my first meeting, I had already purchased quite a bit of property as a real estate investor—everything from single-family and multifamily homes to one small apartment building. I had done this mostly with traditional bank financing on the first few properties and with some creative financing strategies I'd picked up over the years with the rest of my portfolio.

Twenty Units Free and Clear

At this point in my career, I thought I was pretty smart, except for the fact that I didn't call my BHAG a BHAG, because I didn't know what that term was quite yet. I also didn't know that my goal of twenty properties owned free and clear wasn't really where I'd end up. See, in my mind, twenty properties seemed like a lofty idea, a goal I could one day dream of achieving. One hundred properties would be even better! So good, I could hardly imagine it. At either point, I could probably sell one property a year after that and live pretty well into retirement. Now, this wasn't a bad goal—and it still isn't for most people—but I was fortunate enough to hit a fork in the road around ten units. That was the point when I learned that I didn't really need to follow that exact plan, because there might be a better way.

My Financing Problem

As a guy who owned ten units and was doing pretty well, why was I in this banquet hall just outside Philadelphia on a Thursday night in the fall of 2003? It was simple, really: I had run out of money. I had purchased about ten properties in my own name and had hit a financing roadblock. I needed money. *Or at least that's what I thought I needed.*

Coming up in a pre–social media era, I had, up until this point, always operated solo, networking only with friends, family, and the occasional Realtor or broker I'd meet as a part-time Realtor myself. Over the years, I'd heard about a local chapter of a national Real Estate Investors Association (REIA) group called the Diversified Investor Group, or DIG. I never could seem to get around to attending a meeting, but it was always an interesting idea to me. It wasn't until I needed something, when I was without any other options, that I decided to go. I thought I could ask other investors how they got around the financing roadblock that had stopped me cold.

Before I even entered the meeting room at my first DIG event, I noticed a row of vendor tables. Too intimidated to walk in, I struck up a conversation with a vendor, an investor-friendly mortgage broker from Pittsburgh, whose specialty was in residential and commercial loans. He naturally asked whether it was my first meeting and why I was there, so I described my dilemma to him. Needless to say, my problem wasn't exactly uncommon. It's actually why he was sitting at that vendor table. We exchanged information that day, and he ended up providing me the financing I needed to get out of my rut. Problem solved! But my story doesn't end there. I didn't just find some financing and head home. That was only the beginning.

Later on, this very lender showed me multiple ways to access capital, and ultimately he helped me refinance and leverage my properties. I didn't realize it at the time, but my very first encounter at DIG was with someone who showed me one of the powerful concepts in real estate and note investing: leverage.

The Power of Leveraging Connections & Knowledge

Attending the meeting was informative but certainly not ground-breaking—at least not at first glance. Something did stick with me, though: Not only had I made a great connection with someone who would help me solve my financing problem (and met a few other interesting folks), but I had seen what was happening right in front of me: people standing around as if they knew everybody, talking about deals and transactions they had going, and sharing ideas. It was something I hadn't been doing nor had I experienced in that capacity before that night. You could feel something in the air, an exchange of knowledge that was almost palpable.

I didn't sign a contract for a loan that night—or even get exactly what I thought I was looking for—but I knew if I kept going to these meetings, that would change. So I made a commitment to get more involved and to learn. Every last Thursday of the month, DIG would bring in a speaker to educate attendees on a topic, and many speakers would follow up the next Saturday with a one-day workshop, usually in hopes of selling their wares, which could be anything from a book to a course to a full-on mentoring program. I knew they wouldn't all be right for me, but if I attended as many meetings as I could, I would see a wide array of speakers, learn a little bit about nearly every facet of real estate investing, and maybe find a niche to reach my then-BHAG of twenty houses free and clear.

Invest in Debt

When I look back at those first DIG meetings I attended, only now do I see how serendipitous they really were. The first full Saturday meeting I attended may have been the most serendipitous of all, actually. The very first person I got to see speak was a man by the name of Jimmy Napier.

Back then, to me at least, that name didn't mean much. There was no way of knowing he would be considered a so-called founding father of note investing and the author of what is now probably the most famous book on note investing ever written, *Invest in Debt*. During his full-day Saturday talk, he spoke about everything from understanding debt to how to work a financial calculator. I found it all fascinating, but at the time, I just couldn't see myself in that world. I was a real estate investor, and before that, I had been a contractor. The realm of "discounted debt" in relation to the finance world seemed so foreign to me as a guy who was still managing all his properties himself, even doing much of the physical handyman work.

After meeting with one of the greatest minds in the note industry, I did what most people would probably do...absolutely nothing. Well, nothing with notes anyway. I was still dead set on my goal, and learning more about hard real estate was part of the plan. I attended the Thursday-night meetings and Saturday workshops every month, and on the off nights, I went to subgroup meetings whenever I could, building my networking skills and absorbing as much as possible. I kept up this strict regimen of meetings for several years, and it was through these meetings that I was introduced to an endless well of real estate investing strategies and concepts, expanding my network of close friends and acquaintances who invested in all types of vehicles along the way.

My "Aha!" Moment: Everyone Is in the Note Business

There was an "aha!" moment I should've recognized that day with Jimmy Napier, and maybe I did, but I didn't know what it could really mean for me. That moment was this: Napier opened my eyes to the world of debt and how we're all a part of it. In fact, now, when an investor asks me how he or she can "get into the note business," I often reply, "You're probably already in the note business. Almost everyone is. Most people just happen to be on the other end of it." What I mean when I say that is this: Most of us tend to be on the side of the borrower, the one making a payment on a note, rather than being on the side of the lender that receives the payment, like a bank. It's pretty hard to find a person who doesn't have a credit card, car loan, mortgage, student loan, or medical bill payment to make. The best way to get on the other side of this equation is to gain a deeper understanding of debt, leverage, and notes.

Good Debt vs. Bad Debt

I'm not the first person to talk about the concept of good debt versus bad debt, and I hope I won't be the last. How to better utilize debt should always be a topic of conversation among investors and consumers alike. The crux of the "good debt versus bad debt" concept is that debt can be just as helpful as it can be harmful. Good debt is something that can create value, build wealth, and generate additional income. It's often deductible debt, as well, some examples being mortgage interest, student loan interest, and credit card interest, if it's through your business and for your business. Conversely, bad debt does the opposite and is merely an expense; examples include car loans, the majority of personal credit card debt, and most personal loans (unless they're being used to improve or expand something that can create more value or income later).

Many of us, myself included, have fallen prey to accruing bad types of debt. For some of us, it can seem inevitable, like when incurring debt to pay for necessities like education, food, or shelter. Sometimes it's not even the debt itself that's the worst part but all the excessive fees that come along with it, with many borrowers being obligated to pay higher-than-average rates and fees for things like insurance, bank loans, and credit cards because of poor credit or financial standing. I definitely found that to be the case in my early years as a working adult, but as I continued on my journey as an investor, I started to see the light. At the end of the day, debt is really just a means to access capital. Making debt work for you is the best way to remain free of bad debt and build wealth, and one of the best ways to do that is by utilizing notes.

Types of Notes

In its simplest form, a note (or a promissory note, as it's officially called) is a promise to repay a loan. A mortgage is the recorded document that attaches that loan (also known as a lien) against real property that secures the note. A more detailed definition would state that a promissory note is a contract in which one party (the borrower) agrees to repay a certain portion of the loan to the other party (the payee) within a set period of time under specific terms, which could include interest rate on the loan, penalties for late payments, etc. So that's what a note is theoretically, but there's much more to note investing than just an IOU.

With so many different types of debt—whether it's commercial versus residential or secured versus unsecured—it would be an understatement to say that not every note is created equal. You could even go as far as to say that every single note is different and unique in its own way, with different borrowers, lender regulations, locations, prices, etc. But there are categories that all notes fit into. The notes that the majority of real estate investors refer to are secured residential mortgage notes—the two biggest delineations of which are seller-financed notes and institutional notes.

Seller-Financed Notes

Jimmy Napier, and many others who followed in his footsteps, worked more in the world of seller-financed notes. Seller financing (or owner financing, as it's often called) is exactly what it sounds like: Instead of the buyer getting a loan from the bank, the investor selling the property "lends" the buyer the money for the purchase. The two parties then complete this lending transaction by executing a promissory note detailing points such as interest rate, repayment schedule, and consequences of default. These notes can then be brokered and sold in the seller-financed marketplace.

So with seller-financed notes, investors can maximize their profits on a real estate deal by creating a note and attaching it to the property they're selling...or they can purchase a note like this and buy right into it as a cash-flowing asset. This was the world of notes I was first introduced to, and not too long after my encounter with Napier—when I really started to network, learn, and ramp up my real estate business—I would use seller-financed notes to create additional profits. But I don't want to get too far ahead of myself without mentioning the other side of the note business.

Institutional Notes

There are also institutional notes. These are similar in concept, but instead of buying a note that a seller created, an investor is buying a note originated or underwritten by a bank. Through reading this book, you'll come to learn all the reasons why this is the side of the business I reside in today, but if I had to sum it up in one sentence: It's one of the best ways to be like the bank. And why would I want to be like the bank, you might ask?

Banks Have It All Figured Out

In the abovementioned notes, there is one common trait: The investor is not only the borrower—the investor is both the borrower and the lender at the same time. This is one way banks make their money. By persuading everyone to save money for a future need (whether it be out of fear or peace of mind or for a rainy day), banks pay customers a small percentage for this capital and use this money to generate income. The movement and redeployment of this money creates leverage, with *arbitrage*.

In the United States, with government approval, banks help create growth and finance loans by leveraging depositors' money. They do this by borrowing against depositors' capital (up to seven to ten times, depending on the status of the bank and its reserve requirement) from the Federal Reserve (a.k.a. the guys who print the money!) for a fee so they can then lend even more money out to bank customers for an even larger fee than what's paid to depositors. It may sound complicated, but it's simply brilliant. Personally, I think that many people know this but haven't figured out a way to apply these concepts to their investing portfolio.

Jimmy Napier's talk wasn't my first exposure to this idea, just as I'm sure my retelling isn't to you. It was actually my money-and-banking course in college that gave me a 30,000-foot introduction to how banking really works and how money flows through the economy to facilitate businesses, housing, and overall economic growth. This growth is usually connected to new construction, business loans, consumer loans, auto loans, etc.—all of which is finance driven. Once you understand this, it's not hard to see that the facilitators of the money in our society are banking institutions.

How I Built My Wealth by Being like the Bank

Most of the wealth that I've been able to personally accumulate wasn't solely from buying, selling, or owning notes or hard real estate. These things were just a piece of the pie. Where my real wealth has come from isn't the result of any one vehicle but multiple ones—all using strategies employed from *thinking and acting like a bank,* or in other words, utilizing arbitrage or leverage along with other banking strategies that I detail in the following chapters.

Throughout childhood and into adulthood, most of us are programmed to the ideas of studying hard, going to a good school, getting a good job, and saving, all of which translates into success and making lots of money. Well, I studied hard, went to a good school, and had a good construction job, and I still plateaued. Even when I became a part-time Realtor and, eventually, a full-time investor, I had more income (even much of it being passive), but it still didn't translate into the so-called American dream of success. What I learned, standing in those banquet halls full of real estate investors over the years, slowly becoming one of the successful ones, was that the "typical" path wasn't the only way. You don't have to be a high-income earner to become wealthy. The old phrase "It takes money to make money" isn't necessarily untrue, but I feel as if there should be an addendum to it: "It takes money to make money... but it doesn't necessarily have to be *your* money that gets you there."

The majority of self-made millionaires and billionaires in any industry, but especially in real estate, in one way or another leverage people, money, and time to build wealth. For me, this was first accomplished by using banks' money for leverage. Initially, I did this to acquire real estate. Then I used my assets to leverage more money from the bank, raised private money from other individuals to leverage into commercial and residential property, and, finally, through purchasing notes myself at a discount from the bank, really harnessed the power of leveraging money and debt!

I can't completely credit this, and what I'm about to tell you, only to Jimmy Napier, but he was certainly one of the many people who helped me realize the potential of notes. The number one thing about notes and debt is this: Notes are versatile, and there are many ways in which investors can leverage debt and utilize notes and banking concepts to build wealth more effectively, efficiently, and quickly— now more than ever.

The Goal of This Book

Let's fast-forward to today, where I'm cofounder of a company that owns and manages more than $100 million worth of institutional notes and an investor who has exponentially maximized his real estate portfolio to far surpass his expectations of wealth with twenty or even one hundred free and clear houses. After years of attending meetings, watching speakers, reading books, and connecting with other investors, I've continuously tried to take note investing to another level. The majority of my work today is no longer focused on just what my next deal is or where the next investment is coming from. It's on how to make myself and my investment practices better. And beyond that, how I can help others do the same.

Today, my real BHAG, and truly my greatest passion, is to be able to share my real estate experience and knowledge with others so that they, too, can build and preserve their wealth for themselves and their families.

The true goal of this book is to show you how to implement the concepts of note investing, either actively or passively, into your investment portfolio. By understanding the true power of notes and the financial side of real estate, you can operate your real estate portfolio more effectively—and, I hope, with less aggravation. Now it's time to learn to think more like the bank and put your real estate investing on steroids!

INTRODUCTION
TAKEAWAYS

The power of networking. Attending local real estate meetings taught me how to leverage connections with more-experienced investors and gave me access to knowledge and resources (like private lenders) that directly resulted in my investment portfolio and career growth.

Invest in what? What I learned from Jimmy Napier was that everyone is in the note business, but usually as a borrower instead of a lender. Napier's daylong seminar that I attended, based on his famous book *Invest in Debt*, was my first true introduction to the world of financing in real estate.

Good debt versus bad debt. I used to be familiar only with bad debt, or debt that is a costly expense with fees and high interest. Once I discovered the other side of the debt coin, I realized that good debt could create value. Good debt builds wealth, or gives you access to opportunities to build wealth, while bad debt does the opposite.

Seller-financed versus institutional real estate notes. Notes are essentially contractual promises to repay loans. I was first introduced to seller-financed notes, which are notes created by an investor selling the property to lend the buyer money. These notes can then be brokered and sold in the seller-financed marketplace. Institutional notes are notes originally created or underwritten by banks.

Think like a bank. I quickly learned that banks already have note investing all figured out. I learned from them how to use others' money to leverage my deals. I learned arbitrage.

My goal for this book. After years of mistakes, headaches, and some triumphs, I've expanded my portfolio beyond my expectations. I've attended the meetings, read the books, and learned from the experts to get to where I am today. Now, with this book, I want to distill what I've learned to help you build and preserve your wealth with real estate.

CHAPTER 1
How Notes Really Work

The First Note

I often get asked, "What is the note business? How come I've never heard about it before?" I thought the same thing when I first heard about it, and it wasn't until I entered the space that I realized notes have been around long before I ever came along. In fact, notes have been around for centuries. The practice of lending has been traced back to as early as 2000 BC in Babylon, with palaces and the temple acting as a lender, issuing from the wealth they had acquired. These loans typically involved issuing seed grain, with repayment from the harvest. These basic social agreements, along with an agreement on terms and interest, were documented in clay tablets.

Banks and lending have also been documented throughout ancient Greece and the Roman Empire. After the fall of the Roman Empire, it seemed lending had temporarily disappeared from the European region. But not long after, during the Tang Dynasty (AD 618–907) in China, a promissory note called flying cash, or *feiqian,* came into regular use by Chinese tea merchants. The note could be exchanged for hard currency at provincial capitals.[1] They did this to avoid carrying large amounts of money when traveling, especially since such amounts of metal coin could be heavy and cumbersome. It's been said that it was then Marco Polo who brought the idea of promissory notes

---

1 William N. Goetzmann and K. Geert Rouwenhorst. *The Origins of Value: The Financial Innovations That Created Modern Capital Markets* (Oxford University Press, 2005), 68.

back to Europe in the thirteenth century.[2] Modern concepts such as the issue of banknotes and fractional reserve banking developed in seventeenth-century England with Goldsmiths and eventually the formation of the Bank of England in 1695. Across the pond, the first commercial bank in America was founded in my hometown of Philadelphia in 1782. Although today's mortgage hadn't been created yet, banknotes were used, and the modern banking system as we know it took a major leap forward.

The author in front of The First Bank of the United States. Photo by Tom McCarthy. 120 South Third Street, Philadelphia, Pennsylvania. November 2, 2017.

---

2 Marco Polo. *The Travels of Marco Polo, a Venetian, in the Thirteenth Century: Being a Description, by That Early Traveller, of Remarkable Places and Things, in the Eastern Parts of the World* (1818), 353–355.

Just as many people don't realize they're in the note business, they also may not know that these systems and institutions have always been there, evolving with the local economies and marketplaces. Notes are around us in many facets of life. Knowing that all this history is taking place all over the world, one has to ask: Why? Why did these institutions implement these strategies? What was in it for them? What made these notes truly worthwhile? I didn't start to understand the true value of notes, and the principles behind them, until I realized how they had entered my personal history.

My First Note

Back in the late 1970s, having just graduated high school, I decided to make a pretty big decision—I was going to be the first person in my family, ever, to go to college. Being one of six kids raised by a single mother, I thought that my only road to success was through education. Upon finishing eighth grade, I took an entrance exam and was awarded a full scholarship to one of the most prestigious schools in the Philadelphia area: Archmere Academy. To give you an idea, this was the college prep school built on the estate of industrialist John J. Raskob (developer of the Empire State Building) and attended by the likes of former vice president Joe Biden. Needless to say, it opened up another world for me. Growing up poor on the outskirts of Philadelphia, I found this experience life-changing, exposing me to more than I could have ever imagined. Alongside eighty-two other students in my graduating class, I finished just before the summer of 1978. And unlike any other member in my family before me, I decided I wanted to continue my education and attend college.

Because of my grades at Archmere, I had been accepted to three very good schools in the Philadelphia area, but because of severe financial constraints, I opted for a state college less than an hour from where I lived. I enrolled as an accounting major before switching to business management about halfway through my time there. Being a college student who came from below the poverty line was tough. I wasn't even getting by on my menial food service job. I had no choice but to live on food stamps and welfare assistance. To save money, I commuted from home instead of living on campus, taking public transportation and often hitchhiking to class because I didn't have money for a car. All this work and commuting proved to be a big mistake. Paying my tuition as I went, I was working more than half the week and commuting what felt like the other half. It was way too much, and I almost flunked out. By my third year, I'd decided the only way I could continue my education while still maintaining any semblance of sanity was to get a student loan. This student loan turned out to be my very first experience in the note business.

Even though I was fortunate enough to have to obtain a loan for only the last leg of college, it was still quite a bit of money compared with my salary of $3.50/hour at the time. The terms of my loan were as follows:

Loan amount: $5,800

Monthly payment: $65.12/month

Term: Ten years

Interest rate: 6.25 percent

With a lot of hard work and some luck, I managed to finish with a business degree in five years. My student loan let me focus on my studies and live without having to constantly worry about making rent and commuting so much back and forth. I would end up being thirty-two years old when I finally made my last payment, for a total of $7,814.40. It may not sound like much, but to lend a mere $5,800, the bank made $2,014.40. And that's just for a small piece of uncollateralized debt back in the 1980s! I don't even want to show you my son's recent student loan. It makes my full loan amount look like payments for just his first year or two out of college! Now, with a mortgage, the terms and amounts are different, but the concept stays the same—except that for the bank, it may be even sweeter. With mortgage notes, the debt itself is collateralized by hard property, and generally speaking, the average mortgage is for a longer term and larger amount than a student loan. But how much money does the bank really make off a traditional mortgage? I think the simplest way to explain it is by example.

CASE STUDY
THE BEEF BAND HOUSE

Did you ever go to a "Beef and Beer" party? It may be a tradition localized to the Philadelphia area, but I hear it's similar to a "spaghetti supper" in the Northeast or a "pig roast" in the South or Midwest. A Beef and Beer happens when someone rents a banquet hall and another person or group of people donates some kegs of beer (nothing fancy) and the beef. Specifically, thinly sliced roast beef in gravy, which is served on a kaiser roll with provolone or American cheese and maybe some horseradish. Meatballs in tomato sauce will also be found at these events, along with your common deli meat trays, macaroni salads, and coleslaw. Now, why all the food and booze? Simple. It's a great excuse to get local communities together, often friends and families, and charge admission to raise money to donate to a person's medical bills or a local student's scholarship. Plus, generally speaking, working-class people in Philly love to get drunk and eat meat. You may be wondering why I'm telling you all of this, but I can assure you I have a point—a profitable one at that. One that ends in my telling you how the bank makes a killing on your loan.

I'm jumping around a bit chronologically, but to keep things simple, I'm going to choose a property from my portfolio that has a traditional mortgage. You'll see later on how many of my properties have been obtained through creative financing, but even as an investor, I still sometimes obtain traditional mortgages. The mortgage in question was attached to a property owned by a close friend of my cousin's. My cousin hired him to play music at his Beef and Beer events that he organized around town. Sooner or later, this guy played so many Beef and Beers, his group came to be known appropriately as The Beef Band. He was also the owner of the house I was about to buy and happened to be going through a divorce. As part of their divorce, they both agreed to sell their house. And that's where I came in. It goes to show, you never know exactly where the best deals will come from, but they definitely lie with the motivated sellers.

The house was a three-bedroom/one-bathroom twin located fifteen minutes outside South Philadelphia (a.k.a. the hub of Beef and Beers). I purchased the home in April 2004 with a traditional residential mortgage, with the expected use of the property being a rental (so my terms were a little different from those of an owner-occupied loan). They were as follows:

Purchase price of the home: $70,000

Total amount required to obtain the property: $75,327.50, which included closing costs and a 10 percent down payment

Original loan amount: $63,000

Loan term: Thirty-year fixed mortgage

Interest rate: 6.5 percent

I always look at a purchase with two questions in mind:
- How much will I have to spend out of pocket?
- How long will it take to get my money back?

So number one, it cost me $12,327.50 out of pocket on paper. That's including the 10 percent down. I was able to obtain a seller assist for $1,500 and a commission as a Realtor of $1,250, bringing it down to only $9,577.50. The property was pretty much in move-in condition, and I was able to find a tenant pretty fast with market rent being $1,000/month at the time.

Back then, taxes were $168/month and homeowners insurance was $26.17/month. Along with my $398.20/month in principal and interest payments for the mortgage, I was all-in for a total of $592.37/month. Subtracting this amount from the monthly rent I collected, I was able to cash-flow $407.63/month. In a year, that's $4,891.56 total, which meant I would have all my out-of-pocket money back in less than two years, after which I would be making what is essentially an infinite rate of return. I've even employed a few more creative strategies to maximize my profit on this property, and I'll discuss them in further sections, but I'd like to think, with what I explained above, I did OK on my investment. But—and this is a big but—I did this transaction years before I fully understood how the bank made its money. Strictly adhering to the loan terms above, if I don't refinance or sell, I'll have made a total of $143,355 in monthly payments by the year 2034—$143,000 total for lending me a mere $63,000. That makes the interest payments a whopping total of $80,355, or a 143 percent return on the bank's money over thirty years. Now, 143 percent may sound like a lot, but it's really not much over time. Luckily, the bank thought of that, and the interest isn't even its sole driver for revenue.

How the Bank Really Makes Its Money with Your Mortgage

To understand how the modern mortgage really works, its origins and how it developed help illustrate where it is today. The word *mortgage* itself takes us through history. The etymology comes from Old French (derived in Latin). *Gage* means "pledge," and *mort* means "death."[3] So put together, a "mort-gage" is a "death pledge"! OK, maybe it's not that grim—it really referred to the death of the debt instrument when it was paid off, not the homeowner.

In the United States, it wasn't until the New Deal in 1934 that the modern mortgage, as we know it, started to form. Prior to that, mortgages in America were nearly unrecognizable compared with the ones we're all familiar with—most mortgages were for a short term (typ-

---

3 Chris Weller, "11 Everyday Words That Have Weird and Disturbing Origins," *Business Insider*, published March 15, 2006, http://www.businessinsider.com/everyday-words-that-have-weird-and-disturbing-origins-2016-3/#lemur-3.

ically five to ten years) and featured "bullet" payments of principal at term. So unless borrowers could find a means to refinance these loans when they came due, they would have to pay off the outstanding loan balance. In addition, most loans carried a variable rate of interest.[4] Along with the New Deal came the establishment of the Federal Housing Authority, which enacted changes in mortgages like lower down payments, thirty-year amortization, loan-to-values (LTVs) of 80 and 90 percent or higher, and universal standards for qualifying, as well as construction standards.[5] This new set of standards not only helped grow the economy but also bumped up homeownership from 43.6 percent in 1940, the last census year before World War II, to 62.9 percent today.[6]

Conforming and Nonconforming Loans

In origination world, mortgages fall into one of two categories: conforming and nonconforming. What they "conform" to is the secondary marketplace—a market made up of large investors like insurance companies, pension funds, note funds, etc., with guidelines for the market being determined by Fannie Mae and Freddie Mac regulations. The majority of loans underwritten conform to these guidelines, and often they'll sell the day they're originated. In fact, I've even gone to closings for properties I've purchased where the bank has already sold my loan three or five times that day.

If it's a loan that is nonconforming, which could happen for a variety reasons (including a problem with collateral, lack of credit, the loan amount being higher than the conforming limit, etc.), then the loan isn't fit to sell in this marketplace. In cases like these, the bank "portfolios" the loan and keeps it in-house. This is rare with bigger banks, which is why you'll see more community banks with residential loans in-house.

---

4 Richard K. Green and Susan M. Watcher, "The American Mortgage in Historical and International Context," *Journal of Economic Perspectives* 19, no. 4 (fall 2005): 93–114.

5 Green and Watcher, "American Mortgage," 93–114.

6 Prashant Gopal, "Homeownership Rate in the U.S. Drops to Lowest Since 1965," *Bloomberg*, published July 28, 2006, https://www.bloomberg.com/news/articles/2016-07-28/homeownership-rate-in-the-u-s-tumbles-to-the-lowest-since-1965.

The Flip

The loan I had on the Beef Band house was originated with Country-wide Mortgage, a large multistate banking institution. Banks this size usually originate these presumably well-underwritten loans and sell them in packages to the secondary market. These loans could sell for the same price they were originated for, or they could even be sold for above par. A bank would pay more than it's worth for future potential revenue from a loan with what they deem to be a quality borrower. So a mortgage like this at $63,000 might sell for $65,000. This quick return varies depending on the market, the quality of the borrower (and his or her credit score), and the loan itself.

Keep in mind: This small return on the flip isn't all that's going on.

Origination Fees

Although this was a Countrywide mortgage, I actually obtained the loan through a loan originator who was a friend of mine. Most loans are issued through either a mortgage broker (on behalf of banks) or a loan officer at a bank or mortgage institution. At this mortgage institution, the typical protocol is that the loan officer who issues the loan is paid a salary and receives basis points (or percentage points based on the loan amount), or he or she is entirely paid a commission of said points. The amount of points varies based on the institution/brokerage, but I've seen most of these fees start at around 1 percent of the loan amount. So in this example, the loan officer would be paid at least $630 for originating this loan. This fee is paid out only if and when the loan funds and basically pays the originator for obtaining the bank a loan.

There can also be what is known as on-the-front fees for the application or loan processing.

Servicing Rights

So the bank makes the quick return on the sale and oils the machine with origination fees, but it also makes residual fees on the servicing rights to the mortgage. Servicing rights are the rights to service an existing mortgage that are either kept or sold by the original lender to another party that specializes in the various functions of servicing mortgages. Servicing rights can include the right to collect mortgage payments monthly, set aside taxes and insurance premiums in escrow, and forward interest and principal to the mortgage lender. In return for this assistance, the servicer is compensated with a specific fee outlined in the contract established at the beginning of the agreement.

The Truth-in-Lending

Now, let's say Countrywide didn't sell this mortgage, and it chose to keep the loan in its portfolio. Before you, as the buyer, get to the settlement table, you receive a document called the Truth-in-Lending Disclosure Statement. This is a document designed to help borrowers understand their borrowing costs, often including their annual percentage rate, the amount financed, the finance charges, a payment schedule, and any other disclosures along with the total of all these payments combined. So essentially it lays out everything that adds up to what you're really paying when all is said and done. They have you sign this document to express that, essentially, you know what you're getting yourself into.

With a fixed-rate mortgage, your monthly principle and insurance (P&I) payment contractually remains roughly the same for the life of the loan, unless you sell or refinance. What changes from month to month and year to year is the portion of the mortgage payment that pays down the principal of the loan and the portion that is pure interest. The gradual repayment of both the original loan amount and the accumulated interest is called amortization. Along with this Truth-in-Lending Disclosure Statement, a schedule of these payments showing how they change is a required document with your mortgage. This document is called an amortization schedule.

The Beef Band mortgage, like many borrowers' mortgages, was what they call "front-end loaded" with interest. So if the bank were to keep this loan all the way to term, it's not only potentially making that $80,355 in interest by the end of the term, but it's also making a large percentage of that interest up front, along with the fees for originating the loan .

DATE:
BORROWER:
CO-BORROWER:
CASE #:
LOAN #:
PROPERTY ADDRESS:

Branch #:

Phone:
Br Fax No.:

AMORTIZATION SCHEDULE

PMT	PAYMENT	PRINCIPAL	INTEREST	BALANCE	PMT	PAYMENT	PRINCIPAL	INTEREST	BALANCE	PMT	PAYMENT	PRINCIPAL	INTEREST	BALANCE
Beginning Balance: $63,000.00					73	398.20	84.03	314.17	57917.38	147	398.20	125.32	272.86	50252.42
Interest Rate:	6.500%				74	398.20	84.48	313.72	57832.90	148	398.20	126.00	272.20	50126.42
1	398.20	56.95	343.25	62943.05	75	398.20	84.94	313.26	57747.96	149	398.20	126.69	271.52	49999.74
2	398.20	57.26	340.94	62885.79	76	398.20	95.40	312.80	57662.56	150	398.20	127.37	270.83	49872.37
3	398.20	57.57	340.63	62828.22	77	398.20	85.86	312.34	57576.70	151	398.20	128.06	270.14	49744.31
4	398.20	57.89	340.32	62770.34	78	398.20	86.33	311.87	57490.37	152	398.20	128.75	269.45	49615.56
5	398.20	59.19	340.01	62712.15	79	398.20	86.79	311.41	57403.58	153	398.20	129.45	268.75	49486.11
6	398.20	58.51	339.69	62653.64	80	398.20	87.26	310.94	57316.32	154	398.20	130.15	268.05	49355.96
7	398.20	58.83	339.37	62594.81	81	398.20	87.74	310.46	57228.58	155	398.20	130.86	267.34	49225.10
8	398.20	59.14	339.06	62535.67	82	398.20	88.21	309.99	57140.37	156	398.20	131.56	266.64	49093.54
9	398.20	59.47	338.73	62476.20	83	398.20	88.69	309.51	57051.68	157	398.20	132.28	265.92	48961.26
10	398.20	59.79	338.41	62416.41	84	398.20	89.17	309.03	56962.51	158	398.20	132.99	265.21	48828.27
11	398.20	60.11	338.09	62356.30	85	398.20	89.65	308.55	56872.86	159	398.20	133.71	264.49	48694.56
12	398.20	60.44	337.76	62295.86	86	398.20	90.14	308.06	56782.72	160	398.20	134.44	263.76	48560.12
13	398.20	60.76	337.44	62235.10	87	398.20	90.63	307.57	56692.09	161	398.20	135.17	263.03	48424.95
14	398.20	61.09	337.11	62174.01	88	398.20	91.12	307.08	56600.97	162	398.20	135.90	262.30	48289.05
15	398.20	61.42	336.78	62112.59	89	398.20	91.61	306.59	56509.36	163	398.20	136.63	261.57	48152.42
16	398.20	61.76	336.44	62050.83	90	398.20	92.11	306.09	56417.25	164	398.20	137.37	260.83	48015.05
17	398.20	62.09	336.11	61988.74	91	398.20	92.61	305.59	56324.64	165	398.20	138.12	260.08	47676.93
18	398.20	62.43	335.77	61926.31	92	398.20	93.11	305.09	56231.53	166	398.20	138.87	259.33	47738.06
19	398.20	62.77	335.43	61863.54	93	398.20	93.61	304.59	56137.92	167	398.20	139.62	258.58	47598.44
20	398.20	63.11	335.09	61800.43	94	398.20	94.12	304.08	56043.80	168	398.20	140.38	257.82	47458.06
21	398.20	63.45	334.75	61736.98	95	398.20	94.63	303.57	55949.17	169	398.20	141.14	257.06	47316.92
22	398.20	63.79	334.41	61673.19	96	398.20	95.14	303.06	55854.03	170	398.20	141.90	256.30	47175.02
23	398.20	64.14	334.06	61609.05	97	398.20	95.66	302.54	55758.37	171	398.20	142.67	255.53	47032.35
24	398.20	64.48	333.72	61544.57	98	398.20	96.18	302.02	55662.19	172	398.20	143.44	254.76	46888.91
25	398.20	64.83	333.37	61479.74	99	398.20	96.70	301.50	55565.49	173	398.20	144.22	253.98	46744.69
26	398.20	65.18	333.02	61414.56	100	398.20	97.22	300.98	55468.27	174	398.20	145.00	253.20	46599.69
27	398.20	65.54	332.66	61349.02	101	398.20	97.75	300.45	55370.52	175	398.20	145.79	252.41	46453.90
28	398.20	65.89	332.31	61283.13	102	398.20	98.28	299.92	55272.24	176	398.20	146.57	251.63	46307.33
29	398.20	66.25	331.95	61216.86	103	398.20	98.81	299.39	55173.43	177	398.20	147.37	250.83	46159.96
30	398.20	66.61	331.59	61150.27	104	398.20	99.34	298.86	55074.09	178	398.20	148.17	250.03	46011.79
31	398.20	66.97	331.23	61083.30	105	398.20	99.88	298.32	54974.21	179	398.20	148.97	249.23	45862.82
32	398.20	67.33	330.87	61015.97	106	398.20	100.42	297.78	54873.79	180	398.20	149.78	248.42	45713.04
33	398.20	67.70	330.50	60948.27	107	398.20	100.97	297.23	54772.82	181	398.20	150.59	247.61	45562.45
34	398.20	68.06	330.14	60880.21	108	398.20	101.51	296.69	54671.31	182	398.20	151.40	246.80	45411.05
35	398.20	68.43	329.77	60811.78	109	398.20	102.06	296.14	54569.25	183	398.20	152.22	245.98	45258.83
36	398.20	68.80	329.40	60742.98	110	398.20	102.62	295.58	54466.63	184	398.20	153.05	245.15	45105.78
37	398.20	69.18	329.02	60673.80	111	398.20	103.17	295.03	54363.46	185	398.20	153.88	244.32	44951.90
38	398.20	69.55	328.65	60604.25	112	398.20	103.73	294.47	54259.73	186	398.20	154.71	243.49	44797.19
39	398.20	69.93	328.27	60534.32	113	398.20	104.29	293.91	54155.44	187	398.20	155.55	242.65	44641.64
40	398.20	70.31	327.89	60464.01	114	398.20	104.86	293.34	54050.58	188	398.20	156.39	241.81	44485.25
41	398.20	70.69	327.51	60393.32	115	398.20	105.43	292.77	53945.15	189	398.20	157.24	240.96	44328.01
42	398.20	71.07	327.13	60322.25	116	398.20	106.00	292.20	53839.15	190	398.20	158.09	240.11	44169.92
43	398.20	71.45	326.75	60250.80	117	398.20	106.57	291.63	53732.58	191	398.20	158.95	239.25	44010.97
44	398.20	71.84	326.36	60178.96	118	398.20	107.15	291.05	53625.43	192	398.20	159.81	238.39	43851.16
45	398.20	72.23	325.97	60106.73	119	398.20	107.73	290.47	53517.70	193	398.20	160.67	237.53	43690.49
46	398.20	72.62	325.58	60034.11	120	398.20	108.31	289.89	53409.39	194	398.20	161.54	236.66	43528.95
47	398.20	73.02	325.18	59961.09	121	398.20	108.90	289.30	53300.49	195	398.20	162.42	235.78	43366.53
48	398.20	73.41	324.79	59887.68	122	398.20	109.49	288.71	53191.00	196	398.20	163.30	234.90	43203.23
49	398.20	73.81	324.39	59813.87	123	398.20	110.08	288.12	53080.92	197	398.20	164.18	234.02	43039.05
50	398.20	74.21	323.99	59739.66	124	398.20	110.68	287.52	52970.24	198	398.20	165.07	233.13	42873.98
51	398.20	74.61	323.59	59665.05	125	398.20	111.28	286.92	52858.96	199	398.20	165.97	232.23	42708.01
52	398.20	75.01	323.19	59590.04	126	398.20	111.88	286.32	52747.08	200	398.20	166.86	231.34	42541.15
53	398.20	75.42	322.78	59514.62	127	398.20	112.49	285.71	52634.59	201	398.20	167.77	230.43	42373.38
54	398.20	75.83	322.37	59438.79	128	398.20	113.10	285.10	52521.49	202	398.20	168.68	229.52	42204.70
55	398.20	76.24	321.96	59362.55	129	398.20	113.71	284.49	52407.78	203	398.20	169.59	228.61	42035.11
56	398.20	76.65	321.55	59285.90	130	398.20	114.32	283.88	52293.46	204	398.20	170.51	227.69	41864.60
57	398.20	77.07	321.13	59208.83	131	398.20	114.94	283.26	52178.52	205	398.20	171.43	226.77	41693.17
58	398.20	77.49	320.71	59131.34	132	398.20	115.57	282.63	52062.95	206	398.20	172.36	225.84	41520.81
59	398.20	77.91	320.29	59053.43	133	398.20	116.19	282.01	51946.76	207	398.20	173.30	224.90	41347.51
60	398.20	78.33	319.87	58975.10	134	398.20	116.82	281.38	51829.94	208	398.20	174.23	223.97	41173.28
61	398.20	78.75	319.45	58896.35	135	398.20	117.45	280.75	51712.49	209	398.20	175.18	223.02	40998.10
62	398.20	79.18	319.02	58817.17	136	398.20	118.09	280.11	51594.40	210	398.20	176.13	222.07	40821.97
63	398.20	79.61	318.59	58737.56	137	398.20	118.73	279.47	51475.67	211	398.20	177.08	221.12	40644.89
64	398.20	80.04	318.16	58657.52	138	398.20	119.37	278.83	51356.30	212	398.20	178.04	220.16	40466.85
65	398.20	80.47	317.73	58577.05	139	398.20	120.02	278.18	51236.28	213	398.20	179.00	219.20	40287.85
66	398.20	80.91	317.29	58496.14	140	398.20	120.67	277.53	51115.61	214	398.20	179.97	218.23	40107.88
67	398.20	81.35	316.85	58414.79	141	398.20	121.32	276.88	50994.29	215	398.20	180.95	217.25	39926.93
68	398.20	81.79	316.41	58333.00	142	398.20	121.98	276.22	50872.31	216	398.20	181.93	216.27	39745.00
69	398.20	82.23	315.97	58250.77	143	398.20	122.64	275.56	50749.67	217	398.20	182.91	215.29	39562.09
70	398.20	82.67	315.53	58168.10	144	398.20	123.31	274.89	50626.36	218	398.20	183.91	214.29	39378.18
71	398.20	83.12	315.08	58084.98	145	398.20	123.97	274.23	50502.39	219	398.20	184.90	213.30	39193.28
72	398.20	83.57	314.63	58001.41	146	398.20	124.65	273.55	50377.74	220	398.20	185.90	212.30	39007.38

Reproduction of original copy of the author's amortization schedule for the "Beef Band House." Notice payment 84 (Year 7) and payment 233 (Year 19).

DATE:
BORROWER:
CO-BORROWER:
CASE #:
LOAN #:
PROPERTY ADDRESS:

Branch #:

Phone:
Br Fax No.:

AMORTIZATION SCHEDULE

PMT	PAYMENT	PRINCIPAL	INTEREST	BALANCE	PMT	PAYMENT	PRINCIPAL	INTEREST	BALANCE
221	398.20	186.91	211.29	38820.47	295	398.20	278.77	119.43	21770.32
222	398.20	187.92	210.28	38632.55	296	398.20	280.28	117.92	21490.04
223	398.20	188.94	209.26	38443.61	297	398.20	281.80	116.40	21208.24
224	398.20	189.96	208.24	38253.65	298	398.20	283.32	114.88	20924.92
225	398.20	190.99	207.21	38062.66	299	398.20	284.86	113.34	20640.06
226	398.20	192.03	206.17	37870.63	300	398.20	286.40	111.80	20353.66
227	398.20	193.07	205.13	37677.56	301	398.20	287.95	110.25	20065.71
228	398.20	194.11	204.09	37483.45	302	398.20	289.51	108.69	19776.20
229	398.20	195.16	203.04	37288.29	303	398.20	291.08	107.12	19485.12
230	398.20	196.22	201.98	37092.07	304	398.20	292.66	105.54	19192.46
231	398.20	197.28	200.92	36894.79	305	398.20	294.24	103.96	18898.22
232	398.20	198.35	199.85	36696.44	306	398.20	295.83	102.37	18602.39
233	398.20	199.43	198.77	36497.01	307	398.20	297.44	100.76	18304.95
234	398.20	200.51	197.69	36296.50	308	398.20	299.05	99.15	18005.90
235	398.20	201.59	196.61	36094.91	309	398.20	300.67	97.53	17705.23
236	398.20	202.69	195.51	35892.22	310	398.20	302.30	95.90	17402.93
237	398.20	203.78	194.42	35688.44	311	398.20	303.93	94.27	17093.00
238	398.20	204.89	193.31	35483.55	312	398.20	305.58	92.62	16793.42
239	398.20	206.00	192.20	35277.55	313	398.20	307.24	90.96	16486.18
240	398.20	207.11	191.09	35070.44	314	398.20	308.90	89.30	16177.28
241	398.20	208.24	189.96	34862.20	315	398.20	310.57	87.63	15866.71
242	398.20	209.36	188.84	34652.84	316	398.20	312.26	85.94	15554.45
243	398.20	210.50	187.70	34442.34	317	398.20	313.95	84.25	15240.50
244	398.20	211.64	186.56	34230.70	318	398.20	315.65	82.55	14924.85
245	398.20	212.78	185.42	34017.92	319	398.20	317.36	80.84	14607.49
246	398.20	213.94	184.26	33803.98	320	398.20	319.08	79.12	14288.41
247	398.20	215.10	183.10	33588.88	321	398.20	320.80	77.40	13967.61
248	398.20	216.26	181.94	33372.62	322	398.20	322.54	75.66	13645.07
249	398.20	217.43	180.77	33155.19	323	398.20	324.29	73.91	13320.78
250	398.20	218.61	179.59	32936.58	324	398.20	326.05	72.15	12994.73
251	398.20	219.79	178.41	32716.79	325	398.20	327.81	70.39	12666.92
252	398.20	220.98	177.22	32495.81	326	398.20	329.59	68.61	12337.33
253	398.20	222.16	176.02	32273.63	327	398.20	331.37	66.83	12005.96
254	398.20	223.38	174.82	32050.25	328	398.20	333.17	65.03	11672.79
255	398.20	224.59	173.61	31825.66	329	398.20	334.97	63.23	11337.82
256	398.20	225.81	172.39	31599.85	330	398.20	336.79	61.41	11001.03
257	398.20	227.03	171.17	31372.82	331	398.20	338.61	59.59	10662.42
258	398.20	228.26	169.94	31144.56	332	398.20	340.45	57.75	10321.97
259	398.20	229.50	168.70	30915.06	333	398.20	342.29	55.91	9979.68
260	398.20	230.74	167.46	30684.32	334	398.20	344.14	54.06	9635.54
261	398.20	231.99	166.21	30452.33	335	398.20	346.01	52.19	9289.53
262	398.20	233.25	164.95	30219.08	336	398.20	347.88	50.32	8941.65
263	398.20	234.51	163.69	29984.57	337	398.20	349.77	48.43	8591.88
264	398.20	235.78	162.42	29748.79	338	398.20	351.66	46.54	8240.22
265	398.20	237.06	161.14	29511.73	339	398.20	353.57	44.63	7886.65
266	398.20	238.34	159.86	29273.39	340	398.20	355.48	42.72	7531.17
267	398.20	239.64	158.56	29033.75	341	398.20	357.41	40.79	7173.76
268	398.20	240.93	157.27	28792.82	342	398.20	359.34	38.86	6814.42
269	398.20	242.24	155.96	28550.58	343	398.20	361.29	36.91	6453.13
270	398.20	243.55	154.65	28307.03	344	398.20	363.25	34.95	6089.88
271	398.20	244.87	153.33	28062.16	345	398.20	365.21	32.99	5724.67
272	398.20	246.20	152.00	27815.96	346	398.20	367.19	31.01	5357.48
273	398.20	247.53	150.67	27568.43	347	398.20	369.18	29.02	4988.30
274	398.20	248.87	149.33	27319.56	348	398.20	371.18	27.02	4617.12
275	398.20	250.22	147.98	27069.34	349	398.20	373.19	25.01	4243.93
276	398.20	251.57	146.63	26817.77	350	398.20	375.21	22.99	3868.72
277	398.20	252.94	145.26	26564.83	351	398.20	377.24	20.96	3491.48
278	398.20	254.31	143.89	26310.52	352	398.20	379.29	18.91	3112.19
279	398.20	255.68	142.52	26054.84	353	398.20	381.34	16.86	2730.85
280	398.20	257.07	141.13	25797.77	354	398.20	383.41	14.79	2347.44
281	398.20	258.46	139.74	25539.31	355	398.20	385.48	12.72	1961.96
282	398.20	259.86	138.34	25279.45	356	398.20	387.57	10.63	1574.39
283	398.20	261.27	136.93	25018.18	357	398.20	389.67	8.53	1184.72
284	398.20	262.68	135.52	24755.50	358	398.20	391.78	6.42	792.94
285	398.20	264.11	134.09	24491.39	359	398.20	393.90	4.30	399.04
286	398.20	265.54	132.66	24225.85	360	401.20	399.04	2.16	0.00
287	398.20	266.98	131.22	23958.87					
288	398.20	268.42	129.78	23690.45					
289	398.20	269.88	128.32	23420.57					
290	398.20	271.34	126.86	23149.23					
291	398.20	272.81	125.39	22876.42					
292	398.20	274.29	123.91	22602.13					
293	398.20	275.77	122.43	22326.36					
294	398.20	277.27	120.93	22049.09					

YR PAYMENT PRINCIPAL INTEREST BALANCE

ANNUAL SUMMARY

YR	PAYMENT	INTEREST	BALANCE
Beginning Balance: $63,000.00			
1	4778.40	4074.26	62295.06
2	4778.40	4027.11	61544.57
3	4778.40	3976.81	60742.98
4	4778.40	3923.10	59887.68
5	4778.40	3865.82	58975.10
6	4778.40	3804.71	58001.41
7	4778.40	3739.50	56962.51
8	4778.40	3669.92	55854.03
9	4778.40	3595.69	54671.31
10	4778.40	3516.48	53409.33
11	4778.40	3431.96	52062.95
12	4778.40	3341.81	50626.36
13	4778.40	3245.59	49093.54
14	4778.40	3142.92	47458.06
15	4778.40	3033.38	45713.24
16	4778.40	2916.52	43851.16
17	4778.40	2791.84	41864.60
18	4778.40	2658.80	39745.00
19	4778.40	2516.85	37483.45
20	4778.40	2365.39	35070.44
21	4778.40	2203.77	32495.81
22	4778.40	2031.38	29748.79
23	4778.40	1847.38	26817.77
24	4778.40	1651.08	23650.45
25	4778.40	1441.61	20353.66
26	4778.40	1218.16	16793.42
27	4778.40	979.71	12994.73
28	4778.40	725.32	8941.65
29	4778.40	453.87	4617.12
30	4781.40	164.28	0.00
	143355.00	80355.00	

FHA/VA/CONV
Amortization Schedule
2C181-US (11/01)(d)

Page 2 of 2

There are two points to note here. As you can see in the amortization schedule, by year seven, I would have paid $27,719.82 (or $3,959.97 a year) in interest. With the majority of residential property owners keeping their mortgage for an average of only five to seven years, this is a way for the bank to more or less guarantee it makes the majority

How Notes Really Work   **33**

of its profit up front. Meaning, if I were like most Americans and sold or refinanced my property at this point, I would have paid down only $6,127.42 in principal. This amount is the equity in my house at that point, a small amount after seven years invested.

Where the Tables Start to Turn

Also in the amortization schedule, you see that the majority of the payments go toward interest up until about year nineteen. After year nineteen, the equation flips and the majority of the payment begins to go toward principal. The advantage of amortization is that a borrower can slowly pay back the principal on the loan rather than paying one huge balloon payment at the end (which is how it used to be pre–New Deal in 1934). The downside, of course, is that spreading these payments over thirty years, I'll end up paying $143,355 for that original $63,000 loan. Also, it takes longer to build up equity in the home, since you pay back so little principal for so long.

Banks Don't Just Make Money on Mortgages

I think there is a common misconception about how banks work. To be fair, it's not as if there isn't a lot to know. With more than one model going on, you could easily argue there is too much to fully understand, since federal banks can be chartered differently from how state banks are, and state banks work differently from how community banks or credit unions do.

No matter the institution, most people think banks work by paying their customers to lend them money. Specifically, they think that when a person deposits money into his or her bank account, the bank can then lend other people that money with the depositor gaining a small amount in return (interest on savings) and the lending customer paying a larger amount of money to the bank in return (interest on loans). To make money for itself, the bank keeps the difference.[7]

But it's more exponential than that. That's just one of the ways banks actually make their money.

---

[7] Shamir Karkal, "How Do Banks Work?" *Simple*, https://www.simple.com/blog/how-do-banks-work.

Net Interest Margin

It can be quite difficult to understand this part of banking. Banks operate very differently from most businesses because they are highly leveraged, with more than $20 in debt for every $1 of equity. Not to mention, banks don't make any tangible products, and they often offer things like checking accounts for free. On top of that, most people have the process of how the bank lends and borrows backward.

The way the process works, in a nutshell, is this: Banks attract depositors by offering to pay interest on funds held on deposit. They then pool their depositors' funds and lend this capital to qualified borrowers at a higher interest rate. The bank earns money on the spread between the rate of interest it pays out and the rate of interest it charges on loans. This is called the net interest margin. Bank regulations require banks to maintain a set level of capital to satisfy those who have their deposits in accounts so that money can be readily accessed. But occasionally a bank may run low on cash and need to borrow short-term funds from the Federal Reserve. These loans are made at a low interest rate, commonly referred to as the Federal Reserve discount rate. What's unique about this strategy, called fractional reserve lending,[8] is that the bank has lending power on capital it doesn't necessarily have in-house. And it borrows at this low Federal Reserve rate and makes a spread. This system—which expands the economy by freeing up capital that can be lent out to other parties—was also partially implemented because of incidents during the Great Depression in which many U.S. banks were forced to shut down because too many people attempted to withdraw assets at the same time.

Interchange

So that's one way banks make money, leveraging both the Federal Reserve's money as well as borrowers' and depositors'—but that's not everything. The bank is in the lending and saving business with borrowers and depositors, but it's also in the spending business. Americans spend more than they save, and the bank knows this. This is why it got into the credit and debit card business, especially once they implemented revolving balances. So every time you swipe

---

8 "Fractional Reserve Banking," Investopedia, http://www.investopedia.com/terms/f/fractionalreservebanking.asp.

a card at a store, the merchant pays a small percentage of the money to the bank that issued the card, calling it an interchange fee. For credit cards, this is around 1.7 percent, while for debit cards, it is closer to 1.1 percent. Given our consumer culture, it is a huge revenue stream for banks.

Fees

Do you ever wonder how the banks offer all these "free" services? I put *free* in quotes because nothing in the world of banking is free. Banks discovered that to call a product "free" was a great form of marketing, eliminating any perceived monthly fees but then charging small fees on almost all transactions. ATM fees, overdraft fees, late-payment fees, penalty fees—the list goes on and on. In the United States today, the average household ends up paying more than $200 annually in just overdraft and bounced-check fees alone. A recent statistic by the Consumer Financial Protection Bureau states that in 2016 alone, U.S. consumers paid a total of $15 billion in fees for bouncing checks or overdrawing.[9] Along with the interchange fee, these others add up to more than 50 percent of revenue for large banks. In other words: They're charging you fees to use your own money!

How to Be like the Bank

So where do we go from here? Up until now, it looked as though I bought the Beef Band house and the bank made a killing! And that's true—but so did I. Sure, we can complain that the bank is making more than $80,000 in interest alone, along with fees on my mortgage. Not to mention all the other ways it rakes in dollars, whether through net interest margin of depositors' money, fractional reserve banking, interchange, or other charges and fees. But look at it this way: None of us would be able to utilize credit cards or house our capital in a safe place without banks. And I certainly wouldn't have been able to obtain this $70,000 property either, especially with a fixed interest rate.

Throughout the next couple of chapters, I will explain how we can

---

9 Jackie Wattles, "Americans Paid $15 Billion in Overdraft Fees Last Year, CFPB Says," *CNN*, published August 4, 2017, http://money.cnn.com/2017/08/04/pf/over-draft-fees-cfpb/index.html?iid=SF_River.

invest and mitigate the downside risks, the maintenance, and the management as the banks do and exponentially grow our portfolios and business utilizing what they do. We may not be banks, issuing credit cards and hosting checking accounts, but we can all mirror concepts of transactional fees and leveraging interest as a note investor to build wealth or as a real estate investor utilizing notes in our business.

CHAPTER 1
TAKEAWAYS

Brief history of notes and lending—and the rise of modern banks. "Banks" have been around since about 2000 BC, as we've found loans (with interest) for grain on clay tablets. The modern bank has come from a long evolution, from ancient Greece, China, and Europe to the first U.S. bank founded in Philadelphia. So the concept of notes has always been there—you just have to pay attention!

My first note: student loan debt. I was forced to take out a student loan, which was my introduction to notes. I realized I paid $7,814.40 to borrow just $5,800. All the bank had to do to make that money was lend it to me.

Case study: The Beef Band House (a.k.a. how the bank makes money on your loan).

Be like the bank!

The bank makes money on more than just your mortgage. Three major ways the bank profits from your money: net interest margin, interface, and other fees.

CHAPTER 2

Financing Real Estate: The Best Notes Are Your First Notes

I wasn't always trying to "be like the bank." Long before I utilized notes or stepped foot into that first networking meeting, even long before I became interested in real estate, I was just a regular person with a regular job. Looking back over my career, I feel as though much of my early adult years were about trying to stay afloat and, little by little, getting ahead. After college, with a shiny new piece of paper called a bachelor of science in business management, I was ready to tackle the world. I went into corporate America, and I was either turned down or able to find only positions that weren't exactly worthwhile. Especially when you consider the combination of the commute, city wage tax (working in Philadelphia), and low entry-level pay, I couldn't find anything that made sense. Oh, and at this point, I also had a wife and a child and was living at home with my mother. Needless to say, things weren't going as great as I'd once hoped. Wasn't this education I received supposed to be my ticket out of all of this? At some point in college, I skipped out of my fast-food job and found a job in construction. I chose it because it paid $3.25/hour. That was a lot of money back then! In fact, coupled with a few raises, it may have paid a little too much. It made me feel comfortable, and what I did next was probably one of my biggest regrets—I continued on with my day job as a contractor...for thirteen years.

The Football Game of Life

I can't remember where I first heard the phrase "the football game of life," but ever since, I've been using it to illustrate purposeful planning for investors new and old. The so-called football game is the time period from approximately age twenty-five to sixty-five, the working years for most folks. When you're twenty-five years old, you're all excited about the future. Business degree in tow, I know I was. But by about age forty-five, you're like where I was—walking into that DIG meeting that fateful day in 2003, being surrounded by those more successful than I was, and thinking, Why haven't I accomplished more? Then, by sixty-five, many folks are playing catch-up. The one reason I think this happens is that most people don't invest wisely, and if they do, they are either afraid to use many of the banks' strategies or simply don't know these strategies exist. At this point in my life, I was the latter, just entering the stadium. I worked as a contractor during the day, while my wife worked a variety of odd jobs, usually at night when I was able to watch our newborn son. I thought we both needed to work more to save more money and get better jobs. Leverage wasn't even in the equation or on my radar. Heck, I didn't even realize I was just at the beginning of the football game! I thought that was all there was. And sadly, for many people, that's the case.

It wasn't until many years later, after working in real estate and insurance and even dabbling in financial planning, that I understood where I was at that time in my life. Getting to see the entire cycle of people's lives—their business successes and failures, divorces, the execution of estates, etc.—I learned that many of the biggest mistakes people make financially are in the years between ages twenty-five and thirty-five. These mistakes certainly aren't intentional or with the mind-set of planning to fail; it's more like a failure to plan, especially when it comes to essentials, like housing. A small tweak in decisions made about a thing like housing can dramatically change the future of one's net worth, tax liabilities, and cash flow—just by thinking about housing choices in a more intentional way. Although I know I could have done much more, I was fortunate to have done just that.

My First Property

The good thing (and maybe the only good thing) about staying in a job like mine for thirteen years was that I learned a trade. And what my time at Archmere and college taught me, more than anything, was that it was up to me to teach and further myself to move up in the world. At the end of my thirteen-year stint working for someone else, I turned my expertise into a full-fledged business. My mother even warned me that I shouldn't leave my safe job! The job I hated and was underpaid for. Well, I understood why my mother—a first-generation American who grew up in the Great Depression—said that. But after working at a place for thirteen years with not much change, no more room for growth, and not that much to show for it, I thought it would still be worth the risk.

The author's first house and investment property. Photo taken from Google Maps Street View.

Even at this point in my life, I was still under the impression that I needed more income, which in my mind came in only one category: earned income. A few years prior to leaving and starting my own business, I had become a Realtor. Since I couldn't break into corporate America and there was little to no upward mobility in my day job, I thought I'd take on another job as a Realtor to make more money. The idea being, I'd make two incomes instead of one! It's so easy—why didn't everyone think of that? Of course, being a Realtor is commission based, and I learned pretty quickly that my "secondary" income was entirely up to me. I didn't have to rely on someone else to get a promotion. I could sell as much as I could. The other benefit was I also started to learn a ton about real estate. Unfortunately, selling real estate isn't a walk in the park. I went through the usual missteps and growing pains that occur with a commission-based job, but my salesman skills kicked in when I started to get more serious in my second year as an agent.

One of the things I realized pretty quickly was that the Pareto principle proved true at my first brokerage (and probably every brokerage I've been at since)—only about 20 percent of the agents did about 80 percent of the work. And not only did they do the work, but they were making serious money. I decided to shadow those few agents who were successful, and by the end of my second year, I was on my way to becoming the top agent at the company. Even though I was really starting to sell properties, I still wasn't exactly interested in buying them as rentals. Most of the agents at the office didn't do that, so why should I? It wasn't until I learned that one of my Realtor mentors owned investment properties, and was quite successful at it, that my interest started to pique. I implemented many of his strategies when starting out, but one of the biggest concepts he instilled in me was so simple that I can't help repeating it: Once you positively cash-flow after you have all your initial capital back (or if you have no capital in the deal to begin with), you have an infinite rate of return. So keep the out-of-pocket costs low, and you'll be making an infinite Return on Investment (ROI) sooner than you know it.

OK, now I wanted property, but where to start? Luckily for me, my first real estate brokerage was big on education. In fact, the owner of this brokerage was a professor at Temple University and the president of the Board of Realtors. Lenders and other professionals in both the real estate and mortgage industries were invited to teach classes, and all the employees were welcome to join. Much like I was at those first years of networking meetings, I had a voracious appetite for learning. I wanted to be part of the top 20 percent, not the bottom 80.

It was one of those lenders who taught me that buying a multifamily unit is more bang for your buck. As I started to look for multiunit properties, I was thinking ahead. I wanted to buy something with more than one unit, that I could both live in and rent out to others. I wanted to "buy purposefully" so that this property would become a full rental one day. Thankfully, the two-incomes idea started to pay off—not in a drastic way but enough to give me something to work with as an investor. Within this time of selling real estate, I had saved up enough money to finally buy my first property.

Buying Purposefully and Structuring the Best Note Possible

Have you ever heard the phrase "You don't make money on the sell; you make money on the buy"? Well, one of the best real estate notes you can ever get is through buying your first property purposefully. I know because I did this by tapping the FHA mortgage program with my first house. Aside from a VA mortgage, FHA financing has the unique feature of requiring the least amount of cash to acquire a property. And not just any property—you could buy up to a four-family residential property and potentially include rents toward your monthly income when qualifying for the loan (which can expand what you can buy). So as long as you meet the qualifications and are able to live comfortably in a home in your price range, then it's the way to go. Keep in mind: Currently, there can be a limit on the number of doorways investors can put in their name. Back when I started, it was much more lenient, and an individual could have a significant number of properties in his or her name before having to turn to commercial loans or other financing methods. Also, there are other workarounds—like purchasing properties with a spouse or another first-time home buyer—but sooner or later, the best kind of financing (owner-occupied financing with preferred rates and terms) will run out, so use it wisely.

ORIGINAL

MORTGAGE

THIS INDENTURE, made and entered into this   5th   day of   June   1989
by and between
                                        AND

(hereinafter whether one or more, with their heirs, executors, administrators, and assigns, called the Mortgagor), and

a corporation organized and existing under the laws of   , and having its
principal office and post office address in

(hereinafter with its successors and assigns called the Mortgagee),
    WITNESSETH, that to secure the payment of
    Sixty- Seven Thousand, Eight Hundred Eighty- Five   and 00/100
Dollars ($ 67,885.00   ), with interest from date, at the rate of
    Ten & One-Half Per Centum
per centum (10 & 1/2   %) per annum on the unpaid balance until paid, as provided in a note of even
date herewith, said principal and interest being payable at the office of   the above named Mortgagee
or at such other place as the holder may designate in writing, in monthly installments of
    Six Hundred Twenty- One   and 15/100
Dollars ($ 621.15   ), commencing on the first day of   August   1989   , and on
the first day of each month thereafter until the principal and interest are fully paid, except that the final payment of principal
and interest, if not sooner paid, shall be due and payable on the first day of   July   2019
and also to secure the performance of all covenants and agreements herein contained, the Mortgagor does by these presents
bargain, sell, give, grant, and convey to the Mortgagee, ALL the following-described real estate situate in the

County of

    LEGAL DESCRIPTION ATTACHED HERETO AND MADE A PART THEREOF.
        BEING THE SAME PREMISES WHICH   BY INDENTURE
    BEARING EVEN DATE HEREWITH AND INTENDED TO BE FORTHWITH RECORDED
    AT THE OFFICE FOR THE RECORDING OF DEEDS, AT MEDIA,

        RESERVING UNTO THE GRANTOR, HER HEIRS AND ASSIGNS THE UNIN-
    TERRUPTED USE, RIGHT, LIBERTY AND PRIVILEGE OF A CERTAIN DRIVEWAY
    AS SHOWN ON SAID PLAN LEADING OVER PREMISES HEREON TO AND FROM

    THIS MORTGAGE IS INTENDED TO BE A PURCHASE MONEY MORTGAGE
    UNDER THE PROVISIONS OF THE LIEN PRIORITY LAW AS AMENDED.

The author's very first mortgage.

So on June 8, 1989, just a few towns over from where I grew up, I "purposefully" purchased a duplex for $68,000, with FHA financing, and in a decent area and within our price range. It needed some repairs, which wasn't a problem, since I was handy. Usually lenders won't approve an FHA loan for a house that requires a lot of repairs, but luckily it wasn't selling (motivated seller once again!). I wrote into the agreement of sale that I would split repairs up to a certain amount, which gave the seller incentive to accept my deal. I bought the house with a thirty-year mortgage. My loan amount was $67,885, with an interest rate of 10.5 percent and a monthly payment of $621.15. I even got a commission on the property because I was a licensed agent. It was my first experience using what I call multiple streams of income, another technique I lump into this idea of buying purposefully. This strategy is something I've carried on throughout my real estate career and even into the institutional note business.

Residential vs. Commercial

I think there's a common misconception in the real estate investing world that you should try to avoid putting properties in your own name. I understand the asset protection viewpoint to a degree, but I look at my personal portfolio as one of many investment buckets that, if maximized and built out quickly before going on to the next investment bucket, may be more beneficial than risky when looking at the overall picture.

RISK

Whenever I tell this story of my first house or first few owner-occupied properties, I always get asked, "What about the risk of owning these properties in your own name?" For me, it was always worth it, and here's why. The portfolio of residential real estate that my wife and I own is really one of the most important buckets of assets in our overall portfolio. It's been a strong base and foundation of our overall wealth, and I've learned a few things to implement to minimize and mitigate the risk.

No. 1. Titling. How you take title can spread out some of your risk, but it's really about which master you're trying to serve—whether it's estate planning, asset protection, etc. For example, is it better to have properties in a single spouse's name for estate planning, or is it better to own jointly? In my home state of Pennsylvania, to limit potential creditors and risk, it may be better to own properties jointly because this real estate is protected by what is known as *tenants by the entirety.* This is a special form of title open to married couples only (since you file a tax return jointly). You're essentially "one owner" with whomever you purchase, so creditors wouldn't be able to force the sale of the property if only I were to be sued or if only my wife were to be sued. This varies from state to state, and laws change, but it may make sense to transfer to a trust or other entity at a later date (especially if it's paid off) or to add/remove the spouse.

No. 2. Debt. This is a radical idea for some, but not only is there such a thing as good debt, there's even debt that protects you. Utilizing leverage and debt can be one of the best forms of *asset protection.* Think about it: It's hard to take what isn't there. This is a strategy I used often for accessing more liquidity, especially through the use of home equity lines of credit, or HELOCs, against properties we own personally as equity continued to build up.

No. 3. Insurance. When buying personally, my wife and I always take out the maximum liability insurance protection allowed on our policies for our rentals, which insure us considerably. We also employ umbrella policies for additional liability coverage. For a reasonable price, both cover a considerable amount of money in a lawsuit. Also, we utilize flood insurance where required by flood zone maps.

No. 4. Professional management. I've always been a big believer in using professional management. When I started, I was my own manager and bit inexperienced. It was costly, and I learned many lessons the hard way. But I used much of that knowledge later on when I became a part-time professional property manager. At that point, I began seriously managing my properties and the properties of many of my clients. But I wouldn't advise this path—having a licensed property manager or property management company to handle rentals is the only thing I'd fully recommend, since most have a full-time maintenance staff, eviction court experience, etc. Property management creates a barrier between the owner and the tenant much as an LLC would.

This type of strategy continues to serve me well with such a limited amount of exposure. As equity builds in my portfolio, if I don't sell the property and cash in on some appreciation, I can pay off the property and move it into an entity or a trust. I also have the option of refinancing the equity out and redeploying it into an investment that pays a higher yield than the interest rate on the HELOC.

Why Buying in Your Name Initially May Make More Sense

OK, now that you know how to mitigate the risks when buying in your own name, surely there must be other reasons why buying commercially makes sense. Well, maybe not, especially when you consider the following:

- **Financing**. If an investor buys through an LLC, banks will usually lend only through a commercial loan, even for single-family residential (SFR) properties. These types of loans have some major differences in financing terms compared with residential. Instead of paying a 3 percent down payment with an FHA loan, or 5–20 percent down for future owner-occupied properties, commercial loans often require a minimum of a 20–30 percent down payment. The interest rate on a commercial loan is always higher than on a residential loan, and the term is often shorter. Even if the banks amortize the loan as if it had a residential term, you could still owe a balloon payment at the end.

- **Recasting**. This goes hand in hand with the financing and is essentially where the lender chooses to re-qualify you (the borrower) and the property. This can make or break an investment, especially if your financial situation or the property's value were to change, because the lender may re-amortize or even call the loan in full. Lenders can recast a loan or consider recasting a loan every five to seven years. If I had bought my first couple of properties commercially, with all the creative financing I did, and a wacky debt-to-income ratio, I could've been in trouble.

- **Insurance**. This one is pretty straightforward; homeowners insurance is generally cheaper than commercial insurance, which can be two to three times more expensive.

- **Titling**. Well, you don't need to bother with the tenants by the entirety rule here because most banks require a commercial entity such as an LLC to take title—which, of course, has its own costs for setup and at tax time.

Now, that's not to say buying with a commercial loan isn't without its advantages. For one, it allows more creative financing—whether it's private equity for the down payment, closing costs, and fix-up costs or the seller holding a junior lien or owner leaseback to assist the new buyers.

But for beginning investors, buying in their own name can maximize their real estate portfolio growth with more favorable financing and lower out-of-pocket costs. For the deals that I was looking at, all these qualities of owning personally enabled an investor like me to cash-flow more when starting out, which is critical in this initial start-up phase. This investment bucket let my wife and me eventually obtain a forty-plus–unit portfolio at one time in our own names, something that is pretty much impossible today with new lender regulations.

Owning vs. Renting

Although I recommend my strategy of buying purposefully, when considering how I think about buying now, I have a completely different mind-set. When I was young and first starting out, I felt as if I were sold a bill of goods that homeownership was the *ultimate dream*. And I know I'm not alone. This "dream" makes logical sense to me, since this was the "dream" instilled upon my parents, grandparents, and so on. My elders always taught us that the way to live was family, faith, and hard work. "Study hard in school, get good grades, and get a good job." Sound familiar? This was their only solution for providing the best for your family, and after food, the first thing you're meant to provide is usually a residence. With such large families, this usually meant a home that was a good size on a decent piece of land. The theory was, if you lived long enough and worked to pay off your home by retirement, you'd be set. You wouldn't have to make any more mortgage payments, and you'd live happily ever after. I'm not sure what they meant after that. Did they mean live on Social Security? Or maybe live with a small pension? It's not as though the mortgage is the only thing you're paying. Also, what about travel expenses? Paying the college tuitions for children and grandchildren? And weddings? Maybe this "dream" wasn't entirely thought out! I should mention that the majority of people in my family of hard workers lived to only their early 60s at most. I guess this covered them until that point!

Let's stop being morbid for a second and get realistic. With your primary residence, there's one *major* problem with just paying it off: You can't eat equity. It's the sad truth my family had to learn the hard way with my mother's home. She was what they call house rich and cash poor when she reached retirement age, as were so many of her friends. In their generation's so-called dream, they assumed they'd be receiving a pension from their job and decent Social Security, in addition to living mortgage-free. Well, the grim reality shifted with the marketplace phasing out many pensions, Social Security shrinking, and what little she had in mutual funds slowly but surely being depleted in the market (and mismanaged by a financial planner). Not to mention, on top of everything, people are living much longer than they ever did, including my mother. She was fortunate to have her property go up in value, which I could sell for a minimal profit. I luckily took what savings she had that weren't depleted in the market and parlayed it into a sizable portion of notes that have covered all her expenses since. But we learned the hard way, and I'm sure there are others who have it worse. Paying off your primary residence and "owning" your home isn't all that it was cracked up to be.

It's not just those from her generation—most people tend to think that the best thing they can do with their money is to put it toward their biggest asset, which is their home. Most believe that paying down mortgage debt is a great use of their money, while also getting tax breaks and building wealth with the potential appreciation of their property.

Ironically enough, long after purchasing my first property and creating a larger portfolio of properties, I think the idea of owning a home is actually a fallacy that makes up a greater part of this so-called dream. Whenever someone says they want to pay off their property and "own" their home outright, I bluntly cut right to my point of home-ownership by saying, "Try not paying your taxes for a year, and see who owns your property." My suggestion to most people, especially real estate investors or high-income earners is, "Why not rent?"

When it comes to living well, especially in higher-priced properties, I think it pays to rent rather than own. If you want to live in a place like New York City, San Francisco, or most areas in the United States with oceanfront property, it definitely can be a better idea to rent. I have a very successful friend, for example, who travels often and really lives all over the world. One of the last places he lived was in Maui, where he chose to rent a two-bedroom, 1,300-square-foot house not far from the beach. It's not quite on the water, but it's only a five-minute drive to it. How much does a place like this cost to own? Back when he moved in, between $800,000 to $1 million, which may be even more today. Now, how much was it to rent this place? Only about $2,300 a month. If you were to put $800,000 into an amortization schedule, roughly figure out your PITI (principal, interest, taxes, and insurance), and compare it with market rent, I think you'd quickly tell me what's more worth it. Putting that same $800,000 into hard money notes or institutional notes that gain a 15 percent return, you could make $10,000 a month, leaving you with more than $7,000 in disposable cash flow.

I don't think my fresh-off-the-boat grandparents were thinking of any of this when they had that homeownership dream instilled upon them, but it is something to consider. I'm all for owning properties, but you don't have to own where you live. Rather, you don't have to let where you live *own you*, at least not into retirement age and beyond. The strategy outlined above with my first property works only if you can live there, but it can work pretty well pretty fast. And in those pivotal years, during the beginning of the football game of life, you want to make the right decisions that will allow you to rent or own desirable property later. It's all about timing and knowing when to use the proper strategy. If I tried to purchase my first properties like how I live now, getting closer to retirement age, I probably wouldn't own too many! And even after this initial purchase, my strategy started to shift with the times.

CHAPTER 2
TAKEAWAYS

My failed American dream? I was the first one in my family to go to an elite private school and then to college, and I thought a degree would set me up for life. I was wrong.

The accidental benefit of being unemployable in corporate America. I became a contractor! The good news is that, in that time, I started my own business and became a Realtor. This led me to my path of real estate investing.

Buying my first property (a duplex) "intentionally" with FHA financing. Believe it or not, the period between ages twenty-five and thirty-five can be critical to establishing a strong foundation for building wealth. This is why buying your first property intentionally is so important.

Why buying in my own name was worth the "risk." There is a lot of fear about holding rental properties in your personal name. I've shown that through financing, recasting, insurance, and titling, that's not always true.

The fallacy of the dream of homeownership, and a twist on owning versus renting. When my mother retired, she was house rich and cash poor. Her story shows that the emotional payoff of owning your primary residence free and clear may keep you from building wealth by using your locked-up equity.

CHAPTER 3

When Traditional Financing Dried Up Part I

Using Unsecured Notes to Purchase Properties

Unless you're a very high income earner, the number of mortgages you have in your own name may start to become more difficult to obtain as time goes on. I know it was for me. I've seen many investors resort to larger down payments with less favorable interest rates as their portfolios grew in their own names. Obviously, buying this way will usually take longer, since you have to save up the down payment and closing costs, especially if you're trying to do all of this with your own personal savings. Many investors, when starting out with their first properties, may not realize what it takes to own a home. I, for one, didn't know how complicated it would truly get. I probably didn't even think that far ahead, being so wrapped up in each and every new deal that I was capable of executing.

What It Takes to Own a Home

There's a lot of perceived honor and prestige in homeownership, but it's funny how that starts to go away with the more properties you own. It's also funny that the banks can play to this prestige through their marketing to the public. After all, human nature is to care what others think. Sometimes it's referred to as the herd effect: doing what everyone else in the herd is doing. It really takes more than just wanting to own a home—you also have to qualify for one of the bank's home loans. The qualifications really boil down to three main things: credit, income, and your debt-to-income ratio.

Debt-to-Income Ratio

Your debt-to-income ratio is exactly what it sounds like: a means to compare an individual's debt payments with his or her overall income. The more debt you have, or, in my case, the more mortgages in my own name, the less the bank will be willing to lend on traditional residential real estate. This is regardless of how high your credit score is. Also, as you purchase more properties, banks won't count 100 percent of your rent toward your income. After a handful of properties in your own name, they start to count more like 75 percent of your rent toward your income. And after a while, the vacancy factor can lower your income level, sometimes to the point where they feel you're no longer a safe bet to lend to.

Income

This can be another obstacle when trying to obtain financing, especially if you're self-employed, as I was. How long your company has been in business can affect this too. Some banks will consider lending to a self-employed person only if the company has been in operation anywhere between two and five years. Even lending to an LLC may require some seasoning before you can obtain financing. Pro Tip: You want a loan officer to look at depreciation expenses properly. Many loan officers may overlook the phantom income from the depreciation deduction to your adjusted gross income when looking at your current portfolio and tax returns when you're looking for additional financing for a new acquisition.

Credit

Be a stand-up, stable citizen. Have a stable job and residence. Have money that can be documented in a bank account. Most important, have good credit. These are the things our society wants of us? And, hey, maybe if you have all them, then you can get a loan. This may sound tough, but once you get the job in place and you're living within your means, good credit is pretty easy to obtain over a short period of time. Just pay your bills on time. That's what I did, and eventually I had an incredibly high credit score. Only, I didn't have the two other pieces necessary for a loan. My debt-to-income-ratio didn't make sense anymore, and I was self-employed at a company that still didn't have enough of a track record. It makes you wonder, *What's your credit really worth?*

Over the years, meeting investors who have gone through all kinds of ups and downs, I've learned you really can bounce back from anything. Bad credit, foreclosures, bankruptcy. Society has done an impeccable job of making people think that experiencing these things is the end. Credit is just another one of those things we're told are so important until they aren't. Sounds familiar. Almost like my college degree was when I was looking for a job after graduation, or my safe position as a contractor when I was looking to build wealth. Sure, these things all have value, but it was how I used them rather than the other way around. We see the banks make the interchange, the late fees, etc., but what can credit do for us? Most people see it as emergency or temporary money. From the way I bought my next house, I can tell you it's more than that. What credit really is, is a note. An unsecured note, one that you can use to leverage your way into investing.

Buying Investments with Unsecured Debt

This isn't a concept I invented, but I hope it's one that I can teach. As mentioned earlier, unsecured debt is a loan in which an individual borrows money to purchase something and a signed promissory note outlines the terms, such as how much can be borrowed, how it's to be paid back, and at what interest rate. A perfect example of an unsecured loan would be a credit card, where there is no real collateral. If the borrower defaults, the credit card company can report to the credit bureau and pursue a judgment to go after the individual and his or her assets, but, of course, this is no guarantee of repayment. This is much different from secured debt, such as a note and mortgage against a piece of real property or a car that's collateral for a car loan that could be repossessed if a person doesn't make his or her payments. I always knew you should be careful with credit cards, but I never realized they had a power of their own that you could master.

The first time I was really introduced to the concept of using credit cards to buy houses was soon after I hit this financing roadblock. At the time, I was already a Realtor, and within the first few years at my brokerage, I worked my way up to becoming an assistant manager of our branch's office. One of my main tasks was training others, and I was well on my way to becoming a broker running an office. I thought this would be a great way to supplement my income while still selling properties and running my new business at the time. To obtain the broker's license, I was required to further my education, and one of the first courses I took was aptly called Real Estate Investing.

The Real Lesson

I'll never forget my first night in my real estate investing class. It was taught by a popular Realtor and real estate broker who had previously been a schoolteacher. After entering the classroom, the first thing he did was ask, "How many of you have a credit card?" Just about every person in the room raised his or her hand. "OK. Now, how many of you own houses with credit cards?" At this point, all the hands went down. He then took a copy of our real estate investing textbook over to the trash can, held it up for all to see, and threw it directly into the trash. "We won't be needing this." And everyone gasped with the effect. "OK, it's not all bad, but what it can't teach you is one of the most important concepts behind real estate investing: how to buy a property with none of your own money."

Needless to say, we were in shock and he had our full attention. He then proceeded to describe how he himself was buying properties in a nearby town with his credit cards, sometimes sight unseen (other than through a photograph from one of his agents), before turning over the management of the unit to a property manager in his office. He talked about how he had a dozen photos of properties all over his desk, all of which he had purchased with credit cards.

Before I describe his strategy, I should preface with a little reminder of this time period. Back in the late '80s and early '90s, credit card checks were still a pretty brand-new idea to the majority of the public. Cash-advance fees were also ridiculously low, if they even existed. It was almost as if we had access to free money. With this tool at our disposal, our teacher outlined his plan.

The strategy was simple:

- He would find an affordable property well within his credit limit.
- He would write a credit card check out to himself and deposit it.
- He would then obtain a certified check from the bank to purchase a house with cash (essentially enabling him to negotiate a better deal).
- He'd fix up the house with another credit card.
- Next he would find a tenant (creating positive cash flow).
- Last, he would refinance to pay off all the credit card debt he had accumulated.

Keep in mind, before even finding the house, he could estimate the repairs and calculate the payment of the refinance loan. For a property to qualify for this strategy, it would have to be in an area where market rents are higher than the refinance loan payment.

I remember going home after class that night, and I couldn't sleep. I kept playing the scenario over and over again in my head, and I couldn't find any reason why this strategy wouldn't work. Besides, even if the strategy failed, what's the worst that could have happened? I'd lose my credit card? That's not the end of the world. Even if they tried to pursue a judgment, they couldn't take back the property (bad credit isn't as serious as a bankruptcy or foreclosure). The next step for me was to assess how much money I had available through my credit cards. The next morning, I called the bank and had it increase my limits and then proceeded to apply for a couple of more credit cards from a few other banks, all with access to credit card checks, of course.

How I Bought My First House with a Credit Card

The mentor who had trained me in the real estate office told me that every day he checked the want ads in the paper, not just the hot sheet of new listings in the Multiple Listing Service (MLS). I did this with persistence until one day I got lucky and found an off-market deal in the paper asking $19,900 in a neighborhood worth approximately $45,000 to $50,000, with market rent in the area being in the $600 to $650 a month range. So I called and went to see it. Keep in mind, I didn't really have any money other than my credit cards, since I'd maxed out what disposable income I had on my previous investments, my business, and, oh yeah, did I mention in the time between properties we had another kid? Plus my student loan was still being paid back. Anyway, I remember making the guy an offer of $8,000 on his place worth almost $20,000. I thought I was going to have to administer CPR on the owner. What's that old saying..."If they don't balk at your initial offer, then it's probably too high"? But to be honest, this two-bedroom row home needed some work. It was nothing I couldn't handle, but it doesn't hurt to start low. We ended up at $12,000, and after repairs that I did with a friend, I was all in at $18,000 including closing costs.

Here's what I did to get that $18,000. I wrote myself a credit card check for the $12,000 from two different credit cards and deposited them into my bank account. I waited 30 days, got a certified check from my bank, and went to closing. Then I used checks from a third credit card to make monthly payments on the two cards I had already accessed money from and to pay for supplies and some contractors for the renovation work. Next I moved a tenant in for $625 a month, obtaining the first month's rent, last month's rent, and a month's security.

I then went down to the bank with a free and clear property, in great shape, with a one-year lease signed. The loan officer at the bank said to me (a conversation I've had with many loan officers using this strategy since), "It looks like you have a good bit of credit card debt here. If we give you this home equity loan today, we may require you to pay off these credit cards." And in these scenarios, that's when I would smile and reply, "Sure thing, no problem." The bank then sent the money to a title company, with instructions to use a portion of the loan to pay off my credit card debt. The beauty was, now that these high-limit credit cards were paid off, I could use them again!

The bank appraised the property in the mid-$40,000s and gave me a fixed twenty-year home equity loan for $25,000. After the title company paid off the $18,000 in credit card debt, I still had $7,000 leftover. Keep in mind, this $7,000 was mine to use tax-free, since it was essentially a loan. Usually, I would use these funds to improve the property further (by adding a garage, for instance, or building out an extra bedroom, which would also increase my cash flow, sometimes dramatically), or I'd use them for my next deal. Best of all, not only did I have leftover capital to play with, but I still cash-flowed $250 a month! I was hooked.

Next, it was a just a matter of rinse and repeat. I did these types of deals about a dozen more times. My path to financial freedom started to become clear (with my goal at the time being to buy one house a year for twenty years), and after I borrowed the money, made some payments on time, and then paid the credit cards off in full, the credit card companies increased my limits of the loan access amounts! This in turn improved my credit score. So at the end of the day, I basically got the house for free and had tax-free cash in my pocket, and the tenant paid back the refinance loan while I still earned positive cash flow and an infinite rate of return.

What I now realize our teacher was demonstrating was a form of what the bank does with their net interest margin, and that's utilizing leverage. The interesting thing about this form of leverage was that it showed me that I could buy property without risking any of my own money. This was my first exposure to leveraging other people's money (OPM), and if things had stayed the same, I might still be employing this exact strategy today. The core concepts of the strategy did stick with me and have shaped nearly every transaction I've done since.

CHAPTER 3
TAKEAWAYS

The three things you need to get a mortgage: credit, income, debt-to-income ratio.

Throwing the book on real estate investing into the trash can—literally. Perhaps the most fortuitous night in my investing career came when my real estate instructor threw the book on investing in the trash and told us the one piece of practical advice that changed my life.

Buying houses on credit cards is a game changer! Yes, I really bought houses using credit cards. Lots of them. This strategy may not work as well today, but the underlying concept—leverage—is a game changer.

What this leverage strategy taught me has guided everything I've done since. Leverage, leverage, leverage... use it early and often if you want to accelerate your wealth building. Just be smart about it!

CHAPTER 4

When Traditional Financing Dried Up Part II

Using Secured Notes to Purchase Properties

So at this point, I think I'm pretty smart. I've figured out a way to buy multiple cash-flowing properties with none of my own money and little risk. As I continued on with my strategy, I accumulated credit card access lines worth around $400,000 to purchase properties. Sounds too good to be true, right? Well, in a way, it was. It didn't take long before the credit card companies started to charge exorbitant (though somewhat understandable) cash-advance fees and interest rates for credit card checks, making my strategy unviable. Unless I sold something, I didn't really have the personal capital to continue buying property. And the banks definitely weren't going to lend to me now that I was over the number of mortgages allowed for an individual. So here I was again, saddled with the ever-plaguing problem: I didn't have enough money.

This is where I take us back to the beginning of my story, when I walked into the networking meeting that fateful day in the fall of 2003. I needed something to replace the credit card strategy, but I wasn't exactly sure what that could be. Walking around the lobby, I met my future friend and lender, Tom. We quickly got to talking, and I told him about how I had started to build up my portfolio but had run into a wall with financing. He told me that not only was my problem not uncommon but that he had a solution.

What he proposed was something I had never thought of before, and it's a question I have often asked investors since: "What's the rate of return of the equity in your house?" The answer is almost always zero. This was a concept that was right in front of me the whole time I was utilizing my credit card strategy, but I didn't even realize it. Whenever I completed that last step in the process of my strategy, where I'd go down to the bank and show them my property to refinance it, they always gave me the option of a home equity credit line or a home equity loan. I always took the loan. I liked that it was a fixed-rate loan and I knew what my cash flow would be. I also didn't fully understand the credit line or what it could do.

It wasn't long after meeting Tom that we refinanced almost every house in my portfolio. At this point in the early to mid-2000s, property values were climbing. In fact, they were ready to reach an all-time high. The improvements I had made over the years also helped increase property values. I eventually had obtained eleven lines of credit, including one business line of credit, totaling close to $2 million. With the class of assets I was used to buying (think homes under $120,000), this $2 million could go a long way.

Using HELOCs to Build Wealth

You always remember your first HELOC. I know my first home equity line of credit was a special one, meaning it was on my primary and was for the most money! I kid, but it's true. At the time that I applied for a HELOC at the bank, I was granted access to up to 90 percent of the combined loan-to-value of my primary residence. For owner-occupied properties, this is more or less the standard (with non-owner-occupied, it tends to lean closer to 80 percent). This strategy, of course, is best to employ when real estate values are up, and in this case, I got particularly lucky. The value of my primary at the time had jumped to $525,000, which was huge for me, considering I'd bought the house for only $178,000. It was also a big deal because I was able to take out a $118,000 HELOC (a.k.a. a $118,000 second mortgage) at a 3 percent variable interest rate before the market crashed. You might be asking, "Why only $118,000?" Keep in mind, I said "combined loan-to-value," so I still had a first mortgage for $352,000, and they would lend me only the difference. I had accessed the maximum amount of capital, and I wasn't afraid to use it!

I used this particular HELOC to purchase the very same Beef Band house mentioned in Chapter 2 for about $75,000, and it was nearly rent-ready at the outset. I was then able to combine the remaining amount with other lines and purchase an additional four properties within a two-month span. With all the properties, I stuck to a similar formula: Get the initial capital back as quickly as possible (to settle the debt of the HELOC), and continue on to make an infinite rate of return. It's important to note that at this time, HELOCs were relatively new, so they were easier to obtain than they are today and the fees were low cost. In fact, they were much cheaper than credit cards when it came to interest rates, since these loans were secured to a property.

To avoid private mortgage insurance (PMI), which is necessary when you put less than 20 percent down, my investor-friendly lender suggested we do an 80/10 deal with these properties I bought with HELOCs. This is where you get an 80 percent loan-to-value first mortgage and a 10 percent second mortgage (sometimes with an interest-only payment for a set term, like ten years), often with the same bank. This enabled me to cash-flow more because, remember, the less cash into the house, the higher the yield. So when you factor in my 10 percent down payment and the 8 or 9 percent of the total for the closing costs—along with the payment of the second mortgage, which is interest only—this let me have higher cash flow on a 10 percent down deal compared with a 20 percent down deal. Plus I was saving money on the PMI. I also got to write off the second mortgage, since my tenant was paying it back, not me.

Benefits of a HELOC: Asset Protection through Debt

This is a strategy I mentioned earlier, about mitigating risk when buying as an individual rather than buying commercially. I didn't know of the strategy at the time I purchased my first property in my own name, but it's something I've learned to implement on that property and many others in my portfolio. I used it on my primary residence in the example above as well.

Of course, I didn't come up with the idea of "asset protection through debt." Not long after I started getting involved with my local networking group DIG, I attended a talk with an asset protection attorney named Pat Olmsted. She was an expert in estate planning, and she asked a question that struck a chord with me that day: "How do you plan to protect your real estate?" Honestly, in my head, I didn't really have an answer. I never even took the time to really think of it. I was busy in accumulation mode, not preservation mode. Before taking any action, she suggested, the first thing we should do when we got home that day was to take a look at our own situations and assess our risks (divorces, autos, tenants, employees, creditors, etc.). Now, I didn't have any immediate risks come to mind, but it didn't take long to imagine the chance of something happening sooner or later.

In the example of my primary, if someone were to sue me personally prior to my taking out the HELOC, he or she would be able to pursue the full amount of equity available in the home, which at that time was about $200,000. I learned that by leveraging against my property with debt, I could change that. By having my $118,000 HELOC recorded against my primary residence as a second mortgage, there was now a total of only approximately 10 percent equity available for them to chase, which really isn't enough to bother going after. Also in my home state, where I owned the property with my wife, the tenants-by-the-entirety law (remember that?) would make it even more difficult, since someone would have to sue us both personally to go after any asset we jointly owned.

You may be thinking, What about all that debt? Well, there's a pretty simple workaround. With portfolios on the smaller side, as mine was at the time (that is, under $5 million), a fairly inexpensive life insurance policy with a few million dollars in coverage would be able to pay off the properties for future heirs if they wanted to. And that's on top of their being able to receive a stepped-up basis, reducing any of the previous owner's depreciation recapture tax and potentially sizable capital gains tax.

Safety Net Benefits of a HELOC: Liquidity
As the market started to take a downturn, I began to do something similar to what I did with my very first HELOC, and that was to access the maximum amount of cash on my lines. This was to prevent the

bank from adjusting any of my HELOCs downward. I saw it happen once with one of my other lines of credit and lost out because of it. It just goes to show that it pays to keep up with what's happening in the marketplace.

The benefit of the up market is that property values are high, credit tends to be good, and employment is much more likely—all of which looks great when you apply for a line of credit. This allowed me to get the maximum amount of capital to be prepared for the worst. If you worked really hard, paid your house off, and got laid off, became sick, or even retired and needed the money, there's a strong likelihood the bank would turn you down because you no longer had a job or the ability to have one. You could have a $500,000 house free and clear, and the bank may not lend you a cent. So timing with this strategy can be important. This could be even more dangerous if you are under 62 because you wouldn't qualify for a reverse mortgage yet. Your options would be severely limited without doing anything wrong. I've been fortunate to never have been in such a time of need when I had to use my HELOC for liquidity, but I'm glad it's there just in case. That's the beauty of HELOCs—just because you take a line out doesn't mean you have to use it. You won't be charged until you choose to access the capital, giving an investor (or anyone, really) the piece of mind of having access to tax-free capital whenever he or she likes.

Home equity lines of credit aren't the only lines of credit available to the average investor. One additional source of working capital, very similar to a HELOC, is a business line of credit. After I put my home equity lines to work, I didn't want to stop doing deals. Tom pointed out that if I had an LLC, then a business line of credit loan could act as another potential source of money to acquire or renovate property. Not long before he told me this, I happened to have formed an entity for my own investment properties that I later merged with my mother's investment properties that I had helped her purchase in retirement. When I realized I could access a business line of credit from this entity, I was ecstatic. I acquired both secured and unsecured business lines of credit to continuously build my real estate portfolio.

Although requirements may differ from bank to bank, there are qualities in borrowers (and their entity) that banks generally prefer over others. For one thing, banks usually like to see a business in operation for a minimum of two years. A set period of time like this is pretty common for most types of loans and lines of credit. Even when I was applying for a regular mortgage on my second primary residence, I remember, I was turned down for a loan because my painting business had been in operation for less than five years—and the fact that I had worked in painting for thirteen years before starting my own business in the exact same line of work didn't seem to matter. Banks also like to see that the business has filed tax returns and has a bank account. It helps if the account is with the bank you're trying to get a line of credit from. In fact, I've had banks shave a point off the interest rate if I had an account open with them.

The name of the entity is also important. This particular entity had the word *properties* in the name, and although I was able to obtain a line, I found out later on from a lender that banks frown on certain words in a company name, such as properties. The reason is that banks may see real estate entities as an investment shelter rather than a fully operational business. Going forward, I would always try to choose a more generic name for my entities. Lastly, the bank most likely will want you to personally sign on the note, basically promising to repay according to the terms of the loan. While you often have to personally sign for business lines of credit (either secured or unsecured), one advantage is that they usually don't report to credit under your personal name.

You may be asking, What are the differences between a secured and an unsecured business line of credit? Well, it all goes back to the requirements. Depending on various factors, some banks prefer to see this loan tied to a piece of real estate (which doesn't necessarily have to be owned by that entity). This is considered a secured business line of credit. I have one of these tied to a multiunit I currently own. In my case, if I were to default on my business line, my multiunit would serve as collateral. These types of lines are fairly inexpensive to set up, with quick closings, so it's easy money.

The other type of business line is similar to a credit card since it is *unsecured* and therefore not tied to a piece of real estate. Initially I used both types of business lines to obtain a few more investments. Personally, I prefer not to use an unsecured business line on a long-term buy-and-hold. If I use it at all, I'd rather use it for properties that I'm looking to keep only short term (e.g., fix-and-flips or other short-term or liquid investments). One reason is that these unsecured loans could end up being short-lived because of the strict, ongoing requirements that could change over time, with banks often reviewing your borrower status on a yearly basis. This review usually consists of reevaluating a borrower's financials, which can change the terms of the line or even end up in a denial of the line of credit altogether. I've also become wary of mortgage brokers who push these types of unsecured lines constantly or up front, since they tend to be doing so for their own benefit by collecting large fees or points up front for helping you set them up. Many times, these unsecured business lines end up being a much more costly loan than first advertised.

A default on these lines is a big risk. They could take your property if it's secured, and if it's unsecured, you could be sued personally and for any assets your entity owns. Both of these types of lines of credit have their time and place, but it didn't take long for me to figure out I should move on to different types of financing.

The Risks of Lines of Credit

When you're a real estate investor long enough, it seems as though everyone gets in the real estate business. Even my plumber, who was a friend from childhood, became a real estate investor just like me. Obviously, knowing how to do plumbing and heating is a big plus when dealing with real estate investments, since they are two of the most expensive things that can go wrong with a home. So my buddy had a huge edge. He also happened to have a very successful small business for many years and lived in a very nice single home on three acres with his wife and children. He had been pretty successful with his real estate investments too. When he learned about HELOCs, he did what many of us do and tapped into the ones he had available. And also like us, he tapped into the equity in his primary residence with a great low interest rate (much lower than he could borrow from a traditional private or hard money lender), using this money to acquire fixer-uppers and refinance them after renting, a strategy that's often referred to as BRRR (buy, rehab, refinance, repeat).

It was with this HELOC capital that he'd purchased a nice three-bedroom property about thirty minutes from his home. He had started fixing up the place, and then, without warning, tragedy struck. He suffered a heart attack. He was lucky. He lived and ended up making a full recovery. But it didn't happen overnight. The heart attack put him out of work for about nine months. Things got really tight really quick for him. Not only could he not work in his main career as a self-employed contractor, but his real estate career was also out of commission, in more ways than one. The rehab was on hold, and his means of financing were causing major problems. I don't think any of us realized how much was at risk when taking out a HELOC on a primary residence. For a while, it looked as if he was well on his way to losing his family's home. Fortunately, he was able to get back on track and avoid foreclosure, never to make the same mistake again. After witnessing what happened to my friend, I decided the cheaper, short-term money just wasn't worth the risk.

There are quite a few lessons we can all learn from this story—having enough disability insurance in case tragedy strikes, being able to replace yourself in your own business, or even sticking to the rule of thumb of having enough reserves to cover six months' to a year's worth of living expenses. But I also realized a few other things. He put everything into one deal, and a pretty illiquid one at that. Worst of all, this was a deal attached to his most important asset: his family's home. This was a wake-up call for me. I knew that there had to be a better way to fund deals—a way that would not only involve less risk but also hopefully still offer me the ability to grow my portfolio just as quickly. What I ended up discovering next was one of the most revolutionary concepts I've been able to harness to exponentially build wealth, mitigating much of the risk found in most other strategies. It's really a strategy the bank had been using all along.

CHAPTER 4
TAKEAWAYS

When the credit card well ran dry, it was on to home equity lines! Thanks to an appreciating market and fairly lenient lending parameters, I was able to start using HELOCs as my primary source of investing capital.

Using HELOCs to build my wealth exponentially. Tapping into the equity of my rental property portfolio by using HELOCs gave me a capital infusion that I used to grow that portfolio even further.

Another benefit: HELOCs and asset protection. They can't take it if it's not there. Stripping equity can be a good way to make your assets less desirable to an attorney considering suing you.

Market timing and HELOCs—pay attention! HELOCs are a powerful tool, but you can get in trouble with them if you overextend and the market turns.

Using business lines of credit as a real estate investor has its benefits and risks. It's important not to put it all on your HELOC, especially on your primary.

CHAPTER 5

When Traditional Financing Dried Up Part III

Using Private and Hard Money

Net interest margin. What was that, again? Oh right, it's how the banks use other people's money to build wealth. Not too long after I saw what happened to my friend the plumber, I decided to use a very similar concept in my own investing.

Early in my investing career, I had done the same thing as my plumber friend, borrowing against my primary residence to purchase speculative fix-and-flips. But today, I would almost never use a HELOC to buy another property. Most likely, I would use what is known as private money, or a very similar concept known as hard money, to acquire either BRRR or buy-and-hold rental properties.

When I refer to hard money, I specifically mean loans that are backed by the value of the property, as opposed to loans based on the quality of the borrower (and his or her credit). The property itself acts as collateral in the transaction and serves as protection to the lender in case the borrower were to default on the loan. The lender in turn charges points (each point is a percentage of the loan amount), setup fees, etc. Private money is similar, but with a private lender, you may be able to achieve much more favorable terms and rates and, depending on the private lender, more capital for an investment property. The sky's the limit with private money, since there isn't a formalized standard. Not to mention, when you're borrowing with close friends and family, they're bound to be more lenient than a professional lender who's looking at a certain LTV, draw schedules, budgets, estimates, reserves, etc.

You may be asking why I would choose money that costs me more than the nearly "free" money in my HELOCs. Sure, using private or hard money causes a higher short-term rate, and I'd have to find an approving lender, but it's worth it. Here's why: Let's say my plumber friend had used private or hard money instead of his HELOC. It won't take long to explain that things would have played out much differently when his heart attack took place. First, a private or hard money lender usually doesn't report to credit, and the loan is normally just attached to the house being lent on. So if you were to fall on hard times as my plumber did and couldn't make payments, you would not only avoid dinging your credit but would also probably just end up transferring the property back to the lender. That's it. No harm, no foul (although maybe don't expect said hard or private money lender to lend to you again). You also wouldn't be putting your primary residence at risk. All that you would be risking is the potential deal you're working on. When using our HELOCs, we took all the risks by using what was essentially our *own* private money when we should've been mitigating the risk rightfully to the lender.

Beyond the risk, there's also a limit to lending with HELOCs, and leave it to me to do enough deals to find it. For a period of time, I had reached the limit I had available, and although I would have my HELOC money back upon a deal's completion, I could still see the writing on the wall. There was a safer form of investment capital, and not only that, it was a source of capital that was and is potentially unlimited. That's when I turned to my networking group, DIG, yet again for my next strategy. Remember when I said if I had to choose, I'd prefer the unsecured business line of credit? Or how one of the major benefits of credit card investing for me was that I really didn't have much to lose? Well, that led me to my logical next step.

Private Money

I had seen a few speakers over the years at DIG talk about the use of private and hard money. Unfortunately, what they said had very little effect on me, since my zero percent interest or very low interest credit cards were still my weapon of choice. I had what was essentially free money, So why waste my time? I thought. And soon after the credit card strategy shifted, I was then tied up with my own HELOCs that were probably as close to free as you could get. But at this point in my life, I was ready to listen.

I had already begun a journey of sorts into private money as a private money lender. I had lent some private money on a few deals, either from what HELOC money I had leftover when properties would hit that infinite rate of return mark, or I would use some of my retirement capital from my self-directed IRA. But for some reason, I never thought to use that type of money for my own deals. The next deal I found was a bit out of my price range, so I knew I would need a private investor.

Where did I find that willing lender? My good friend Steve, who is a very successful private lender himself, has a great saying I like to use when talking about finding private money. He says the first place everyone should start to look for private money is inside his or her cell phone. And what he means by that is the contacts of your current network. Friends and family are usually at the top of the list, and I went right to the most successful ones, the first being my cousin Mike. Mike had a very successful career at one of the country's leading energy companies, and both he and his wife were high-income earners who had capital to invest. Like most people, even many high-income earners, they didn't have a readily available investment that could net them a decent return. My cousin knew of my track record and my strategy with the buildings I had either flipped or kept in my portfolio, so he agreed to stake me on my next deal.

Why Private Money Can Beat a Joint Venture

With my experience today, I see common patterns in how the typical real estate investor does a deal. For example, a lot of new investors would rather start out with a multifamily property instead of an SFR property, when it usually makes much more sense to do it the other way around, if possible. I think this mind-set goes back to either inexperience or the fear of "How do I pay the mortgage if I have a vacancy?" I think the same goes for using private money, with many newbie real estate investors gravitating toward a partnership on their deals because they're afraid of the scenario of *"How do I pay the private money investor back if the deal goes south?"* I know this because I thought this way, and I nearly formed a partnership at this point in my career on this particular deal with my cousin.

Before I dispel the entire idea of a partnership, I can't say there aren't advantages, because there certainly are. A partner could bring a different skill set to the table and may be able to share the workload and provide other resources. A partnership can also cut the perceived risk in half. But along with that can come some potential problems, especially if the *roles and responsibilities* and the *compensation* aren't well defined early on. I know this because I had partnered once before early in my career.

Without my getting too offtrack, my story is one that serves as a reminder for me and hopefully as a precautionary tale to you that partnerships can be much more difficult than simply borrowing private money. One of my first partnerships started when a buddy of mine called me up to do a deal he'd found off market, privately in the newspaper. It was a house that had burned down a few blocks from my then-current home (which was the duplex I bought in Chapter 3). My friend was a carpenter who framed houses at the construction site where I'd worked as a painting contractor. He knew I dabbled in real estate and had a license, so I think that's why he called me when he found the deal. Upon seeing the property, we didn't hesitate to buy the shell for about $16,000; we were all in for $18,000 total with closing costs. I put most of my half of the $18,000 on a credit card. Since I was a Realtor, I handled all the paperwork for free. Then we proceeded to fix up the fire job, and let's just say the work involved probably made it my last property with fire damage I would ever acquire. Have you ever tried to get smoke damage off brick? I wish I could say, "Me neither!" Anyway, the deal my partner and I had was that he would obtain an estimate, I'd get an estimate, and then we'd get an outside third party to give us another estimate. This type of head-butting decision making slowed us down big time. I could think of a dozen or so examples that led to this project's taking about a year to complete. It could've easily been done in about six months without the two of us trying to come up with separate solutions because I could have made all the decisions on my own much more quickly. It was like working on a construction site that didn't have a superintendent.

Long story short, when it was all said and done, this type of partnership ended up being my last. It really all came back to this control and decision-making issue, especially when it came time to sell. My partner had insisted on selling the property, and in my opinion as a Realtor, we were in a buyer's market at that time, meaning it would be an uphill battle. Being a single guy with few investments and liabilities to worry about, he could afford the monthly hit of holding the property vacant. But I couldn't do that as a small business owner with a family to provide for. I ended up buying him out with a refinance loan and then moving my family into the property. We stayed in the house for the next two years and then proceeded to rent it out for several years, before flipping it out for a profit when the market got better.

Today, my former partner and I are still friends, but I can see how some partnerships that go through similar scenarios don't end as well. So word to the wise: Have your goals in alignment and your roles, responsibilities, and compensation well defined before starting a partnership. And don't forget to have a plan B!

Anyway, where was I? Oh, that's right. I was about to tell you how I narrowly avoided a similar, possibly even more unfortunate situation by not partnering with my cousin. As is often the case with partnerships, each person brings something to the table. Each also lacks things the other partner has. For example, my cousin wasn't very handy, but he had plenty of capital to deploy, whereas I didn't. Yet both of us wanted to invest in real estate. This is how it shook out.

The Deal

All deals start somewhere. This one happened to start as an inherited property that found it's way to me through a car wash. OK, let me demystify that last statement. Until this point in my career, I had fairly consistent access to capital—first through my credit cards, then through my HELOCs, and pretty soon I was about to have it with private money. There are really two things you need to make real estate investing work: access to cash and access to deals. Seeing as I had one (the capital), I had gotten pretty creative with the other (the deals). I had word-of-mouth referrals, newspaper ads (this was pre-internet), "bandit" signs, direct mail marketing to motivated sellers (e.g., out-of-state owners, divorcees, executors of estates, etc.)—you name it! But this one came to me from a simple gesture I probably thought nothing of. I had business cards as a Realtor, and on the back of these cards, I had a typical "We Buy Houses—Any Condition, Any Type" sort of ad on the back. I would often hand these cards out, and I suppose I posted one on the corkboard at a nearby car wash. One day I received a call from a motivated seller, two in fact, claiming they'd seen my ad there. They were brothers who lived in Florida and were in possession of their late sister's home. I didn't even have the private money lined up at the time, but I still went to check it out.

Needless to say, it was a steal. And not only that, it was a huge step up for me at this point, since it was located on the Main Line. For those of you who are unfamiliar, this is a famous western suburb of Philadelphia that is historically known as one of the so-called bastions of "old money" in the northeastern part of the country. The place I ended up purchasing cost only $160,000 to acquire and was in need of $40,000 in necessary renovations. I had enough capital to pay for the renovations, but I did need the acquisition money, and that's when I approached my cousin. Of course, this is when he asked me whether I wanted to split the deal with him. After all, without him, I wouldn't be able to get the deal. And half a deal is better than no deal at all, right? Well, this time I said no for a variety of reasons, and here's why:

First of all, in this case, I had found the deal and personally completed all the real estate and title work on it. Because of my renovation background, I also wound up doing all the supervising of subcontractors, scheduling, and cleaning. I also pulled all the permits and got estimates, and on top of all of that, I personally painted the property myself for no cost. This doesn't include the process of listing the property myself or obtaining the refinancing when the project was complete. My cousin is and was employed in a full-time job and couldn't possibly fulfill all the demands necessary to get the property up to par. So if we had agreed to a partnership, I clearly would've been taking on a lot more than an equal share of the workload. But it's not just the disproportionate amount of work that would've been troublesome. With how the deal would've shaken out if we had been partners, I really would've been getting the short end of the stick.

Looking at the details of the deal, this is how it would've ended up had we been partners:

Cost of the property: $160,000

Fix-up costs: $40,000

Total cash into the deal: $200,000

After-repair value: $320,000

Total equity: $120,000

Realtor commission fee (6 percent) + transfer tax (1.25 percent): $23,200

Total approximate net proceeds to each partner: $96,800/two partners = $48,400

After taxes (i.e., approximately 30 percent tax if sold in less than one year): $33,880 each

So $33,880 for all that work I had put into that property. That didn't seem quite worth it to me. So instead, I had the foresight to tell my cousin I would rather use private money on this deal (specifically, *his* private money), if he were interested, of course. That way, not only would the roles and responsibilities be agreed on up front, since he's just the money partner, but so would the fee structure (i.e., we're no longer splitting profits fifty-fifty). The numbers still worked for me, so he chose to lend me the $160,000 at 13 percent for one year, interest only, with a two-point prepayment penalty if I paid him off in less than six months. His private money loan to me was secured with a note and mortgage, plus a deed in lieu of foreclosure, in case I were ever to default.

So with the same property, the same amount of workload for me, and no partner, this is how the numbers turned out:

Cost of the property: $160,000

Fix-up costs: $40,000

Total cash into the deal: $200,000

After-repair value: $320,000

Total equity: $120,000

Cost for one year's private money: $20,800

Net proceeds to me before taxes: $99,200

Minus approximately $19,200 (6 percent) for Realtor fees + $4,000 (1.25 percent transfer tax): $76,000

After taxes (i.e., approximately 30 percent tax if sold in less than one year): $53,200

After taxes (i.e., approximately 15 percent tax if sold in more than one year): $64,600

Upon completion of the renovations, I ended up refinancing the property and rented it to a doctor completing her residency in Philadelphia. I held the property for several years before selling it on a lease option (more on that later), but the moral of the story is that I would've given up a significant portion of my deal (at least $19,320 in short-term gain) and the net profits. The lesson for me here was that capital is worth points, and that's it. If you're paying more than that, then you're probably paying too much.

How to Protect Your Private Money Deal

After I had completed this deal with my cousin, we ended up doing many more together. In fact, he still invests with me today and has even introduced me to other investors looking to do the same. It goes to show that the best advertising is a happy customer. What's great is, as I continued obtaining properties, whenever I found a deal, I knew all I had to do was present it to my private money list. Aside from mitigating many of the risks I explained in the story with my friend the plumber, I think the biggest advantage to private money is the ease with which it can be obtained once you find a reliable private money lender or lenders. The reason being that once you're in a rhythm, have proved yourself, and have built trust, an individual investor is much more flexible with lending compared with a bank or even a traditional hard money lender. Just about all the terms are negotiable, and the guidelines tend to be less strict because the lenders don't have a large group of investors or shareholders to answer to. Once most private money lenders get started, they, too, are quickly hooked and can sometimes even seem frustrated when they are paid back on a deal and have to wait on the sidelines for the next one to come along.

But finding the deal and finding the lender aren't the only things to consider when using private money. After completing many private money deals, I learned there are a few safeguards that should be put in place to protect both you and your investor:

No 1. Document your deal. Usually one of my first private loan conditions is to have the right documents—like a note, a mortgage, and a deed in lieu of foreclosure—drawn up by an attorney or a title company. In my home state of Pennsylvania, most serious private and hard money lenders will lend to a nonowner occupant only who has an LLC that takes title to the piece of real estate being purchased. This is done for two reasons: first, to avoid state *usury laws*, which can be accomplished because there are no interest rate limitations on a commercial loan, thus the reason for the LLC. And second, the nonowner occupant requirement allows the lender to enforce the recording of the escrowed deed-in-lieu after two missed payments (the minimum requirement in Pennsylvania), thus avoiding the lengthy foreclosure process (especially in my judicial state). Personally, whether I am a borrower or a lender, I'm usually doing business with someone I know well. If for some reason you don't know the other party, additional documentation such as a power of attorney or a confession of judgment may put you more at ease.

No 2. Value. You must be dialed in on the property value, both current as well as the future after-repair value (ARV). For me, this is pretty easy, since I do business only in the county where I grew up and have been a Realtor for more than 30 years. Not to mention, the majority of the properties I lend and borrow on fit a pattern, and many of the houses exist in row homes, mostly under 1,500 square feet. I can pretty much tell you an accurate ARV just by looking at a photo of a place in my area. I often say, it's never a bad idea to work with what you know, and if you don't know it, learn it! That being said, this still may not be the case for everyone, and in areas with vastly different comps, you can simply require a third-party appraisal to be completed prior to funding.

No. 3. Insurance. The lender should be named insured on the property and have the borrower send a copy of the binder or declaration page from his or her insurer for verification. This acts as protection in case of an insurance claim, for a fire, for instance.

No. 4. Know the property (and educate the lender). Lenders should be comfortable with properties they lend on, since there is a chance they may have to take the property back. Most of the properties that professional lenders lend on have a 65 percent amount of loan-to-value, which leaves plenty of equity to protect the lender in the event of a default.

No. 5. Borrower's experience level. A renovation track record is key. Think about what would make you feel comfortable lending on this deal. Since the majority of these loans go toward renovations, someone with experience renovating this type of property would make the ideal borrower. In my experience, the best borrowers seem to be owners of multiple properties who have worked in one of the many renovation trades themselves.

No. 6. Title. As a borrower, do a title search, and make sure you have a clear title upon purchasing. As a lender, consider obtaining title insurance for additional protection as a first-position lien holder to avoid any title claims. The borrower also has the option of insuring himself or herself with owner's coverage.

Having a checklist of requirements such as these makes for smoother transactions. Not to mention, with a quality yield that's backed by real estate, these safeguards can make private money lenders feel warm and fuzzy, knowing they've invested with you, and may even make them more inclined to give you more capital.

How to Find Private Money

Looking back, I think this deal served as inspiration for me because it showed me that I could still do real estate with none of my own money. Now, I get that most of us don't have a millionaire waiting around the corner dying to lend us money, and many of us might not even have a network of friends and family capable of investing right out of the gate. After raising money for years from private investors, I'm almost plagued with the question, "Where do you find your capital?" Truth be told, there's really no secret. If you're a reputable and trustworthy person, and you have a viable investment that you can explain (especially one you have a track record of working with), the money seems to find you. But where does that money come from exactly?

Well, it can really come from anywhere. I've had investors utilize personal savings or HELOCs, and I've even had investors who've experienced a so-called windfall of money after they've sold a valuable asset of theirs, like their primary residence or one of their businesses. But outside these windfalls, which could also include inheritances or even tax returns, it's rare that I meet people with plenty of ordinary capital to invest. But there is one area that nearly every working adult has that they rarely tap into, at least in terms of using it to its full potential, and that's their retirement capital. One of the biggest sources of capital for me and my real estate investment dealings has been the use of my own personal IRA and, even more important, the use of others' IRA capital.

Self-Directed Accounts

I was first introduced to self-directed IRAs through my local REIA meeting, DIG. I had obviously heard of IRAs, but I didn't know how to use them properly quite yet. Later on, I found out that was probably because only a very small percentage of retirement accounts are self-directed; currently it's approximately 2 percent.[10]

Traditionally, most folks set up their IRA with a custodian, which may be a bank, insurance company, or stock brokerage. Through these custodians, they can invest in whatever investment vehicle the custodians have to offer. Often, this means stocks and bonds.

---

10 James Sterngold, "Self-Directed IRAs: Risky? Smart? Or Both?" *MarketWatch*, published May 27, 2013, https://www.marketwatch.com/story/self-directed-iras-risky-smart-or-both-2013-05-27.

I'm not like many hard real estate investors, who scoff at putting money into the market. I think there's a time and place for every investment, but the beauty of self-directed accounts is that, unlike a common 401(k) investment in a mutual fund, an investor has full control. With self-directed IRAs, you can invest in many things, including real estate, notes, tax liens, and private placements, as well as traditional investments. The list is almost infinite, except for a short list of things the IRS excludes, including collectables, certain currency, alcoholic beverages, and life insurance policies (but that's pretty much it). Finding this one tool was one of the most powerful wealth-building strategies I've ever encountered because not only did it help me build my own retirement account by investing in what I know best, but it also let me show and teach others this concept. Now I have access to a potentially limitless source of capital. Plus this is different from borrowing traditional money, since the term isn't as important considering most people don't need this capital back until they retire. That could be anywhere from twenty to even forty years after the initial investment.

A Bird Dog Putting My IRA to Work

As I continued going to REIA networking meetings, I, of course, developed a network. This network included vendors, clients to sell houses to and for (as a Realtor), and even people to find me properties. This line of work specifically is often referred to as wholesaling, with the nickname in many investor circles for wholesalers being bird dogs. As a traditional bird dog retrieves the hunt, a wholesaling bird dog retrieves the deal. A young man I was mentoring at the time, who came from a lower-income background much as I did, had taken initiative and offered to be my bird dog. So anytime my friend was working on a deal or found a deal through his marketing, he would present it to me, and I'd ask myself: Where does this deal fit? Would I want to buy his contract for myself? Do I fix and flip, or flip and rent? If not, would my friend the bird dog need a loan so he could do a similar strategy as a budding investor himself? Or would he just want transactional funding (i.e., money to close the deal so he could turn around and sell it to someone else)?

No matter the scenario, it was as if I had become his personal private bank. At the time, I was just starting to use private money for my own deals, and the capital I would utilize to lend was coming from either my HELOCs or my IRAs. One day he presented me with a deal on a property that I personally wasn't interested in buying, largely because it didn't fit my buy-and-hold parameters of a place I wanted to manage. The numbers made sense for me to lend on it, though, so I decided to lend him the private money to do the deal himself. Here were the terms of the deal:

Original note: $10,000

Original date: May 17, 2016

Payment: $125 a month

Rate: 15 percent interest only

Fair market value: $32,000

Rent: $625 a month

First mortgage owned in a Roth IRA

Term: 120 months, two-point prepayment penalty if paid off in less than six months

Maturity: July 2016

I had my title company's attorney draw up the paperwork (which included the note, mortgage, deed-in-lieu, etc.). I knew the value of the property, since I'd been a Realtor in the county where the property was located. I was named insured on the borrower's insurance policy as a safeguard, and I had my friend (the borrower) take out a title insurance policy as an additional precaution. On doing so, I funded the $10,000 deal from my self-directed IRA. It was $9,500 because my fee was 15 percent interest only with five points, or $500. You might be thinking, Wow that's expensive money, but the borrower's payment to me was only $125 a month in principal and interest. Granted, he still had to cover taxes and insurance, but remember he was collecting

$625 a month in rent. When all was said and done, my young friend managed an infinite rate of return right up until it was just before maturity, when he refinanced and paid me off. So the deal was a win-win for us. He was able to purchase this cash-flowing investment with no money into the deal, and I was able to get a nice return inside my retirement account tax-free.

This was just one of many deals I've done with my wholesalers that involve my IRA. Personally, I usually enjoy doing flips and institutional notes with my IRAs because they are typically more passive and involve less paperwork than, say, owning a buy-and-hold piece of real estate. Flips in particular are a great way to really juice your account. Once, my IRA bought a deal for $40,000 and flipped it for $80,000 in less than six months. A $40,000 profit, tax-free, isn't bad in my book! There was another instance when my IRA bought a house, rehabbed it, and sold it with owner financing to my wholesaler friend for him to keep as a buy-and-hold property. A creative solution for both us, and not a bad return either. But I don't even consider either of these to be the best deal we've done together. The best deal my IRA ever funded was for the same wholesaling friend on a house he'd managed to purchase for only $2,500! Now, that's not even the craziest part. What's insane is that he sold the very same property, without even so much as touching it, two weeks later for $32,000! All on a deal he didn't have a cent into. He really hit it out of the park on that deal. I didn't do too bad either, making $1,000 in two weeks for lending only $2,500. That's a 40 percent return over the course of year, but when you amortize that type of return into just a two-week span, it's off the charts! That was a grand slam if I ever saw one.

From these few examples, I hope you see the power of the returns that can be made either tax-free or tax-deferred inside your IRA and other custodial accounts (i.e., Roth, 401[k], CSA, HSA, ESA, SEP, simple, etc.). Remember there may be a limit on how much money you can contribute each year to one of these accounts, but there's no limit on what you can make, or make on an individual investment, inside the account. This was a concept that took some time to wrap my mind around, but once I did, I invested in nearly everything I could get my hands on, from hard real estate to starting a high-frequency day-trading stock fund.

Things to Consider as a Private Money Lender

I can't talk about all the benefits of private money without talking about some risks and precautions. First and foremost, if you decide to become a private money lender, you should always be mindful of not only how much money is given but also how much is given at what time. For example, if there's a very large renovation to be done, don't disperse all the proceeds until sections of the work are completed, thus creating a draw schedule, which is money released by the lender as stages of renovation are completed. Along that same line, be sure to do reinspections, as well, to confirm that all work has been completed before a particular phase is satisfactory enough for the borrower to receive the next draw of capital. Nothing is worse than a borrower blowing the money because he or she is over budget or has used the money for another deal. I also think it helps to have strict timelines. I've found that the best renovators will tend to stick to a very strict schedule anyway. One of your biggest risks is a bad contractor who runs off with the money or materials without completing the project. Some lenders put a full mortgage against the property with only a partial disbursement at closing and additional draws paid as the work is completed, but I've seen others who have the title company make the draw checks made out to both parties, borrower and lender, to ensure that all the work is completed for each phase before the lender signs off. Either way, this is one precaution that you should not overlook.

Other than a contractor/borrower not completing a rehab, there is also the risk of a borrower not being able to sell or refinance the property when the project is completed. This is usually when a short-term loan starts to turn into more of a long-term deal. The more experienced you are, the less likely you will be to lend on deals like these. But hey, anything could happen. The same goes for property that is rented out as a means to pay the loan but is damaged in the process by a bad tenant before the renovator has paid you back. In most cases, if you're taking a property back at 65 percent of value, you're usually pretty safe. It's important to note that these situations are the exception and not the norm, but you should still consider them. And sometimes, especially when you're doing deals like these in large volume with multiple parties, a mishap here and there is just the cost of doing business. I'll still take those odds over losing money in a mutual fund—where I have little or no control, let alone collateral—any day.

As for borrowers, there can be disadvantages in similar situations as well. If the borrowers don't complete a BRRR or sell a property in the expected time frame, they stand to not gain any money on the deal until they do. They can even lose money if they choose to wait it out, since they have to keep paying the private money and the high rates until they refinance or sell. Now you know why I like being a private money lender so much—this constraint is on the borrower and not me!

Plus, as the lender, I'm not saddled with the property at this point, just the paper behind it. I could manage a lot more deals like this, compared with being in possession of each and every property, even with a property manager in place. I know because I was still busy doing that very job managing my own growing portfolio of residential units. But it got me thinking: Being the money partner was a lot less aggravation. This was probably my first "aha!" moment when it came to recognizing the benefits of notes. Even though I didn't know about the note industry yet.

Besides, I wasn't quite ready to drop hard property investing and go right into being a lender. Mainly because I still needed more money to lend! I had also recently dissolved my contracting business because of a back injury and needed to make money as an investor to survive. At this very same point in my career, I had also just approached $1 million in equity. I knew I could access that for 4 percent on average for up to 80 percent of the value in my portfolio, which in turn would give me access to $800,000. With my growing network, I also knew I could lend that money out at the going rate of 14 percent with zero points. That means I stood to make a 10 percent spread on my $800,000, or approximately $80,000 a year. Much better than my first full-time job at $3.25/hour! But not quite enough to make ends meet. I also knew that if I could get more units, sooner or later, I would have access to $2 million in equity. And using the same logic, I would be at an extra $160,000 a year in no time! Not only would I be making money lending it out, but I had also built an ever-growing list of money lenders to borrow from. Essentially I realized I could be doing twice as many deals as ever before as a borrower and a lender simultaneously, all because of private money.

This sort of lending I was doing found me money for my deals. I was getting word-of-mouth referrals as a borrower from people like my cousin, but I was also being discussed as a lender. When people hear you know how to lend money, they want to give you money to invest. It's sort of similar to what I learned later in my career when getting into commercial real estate. I was raising larger and larger amounts of capital, and one of the best ways I did it was by teaching people how to raise money. People like to invest with those they trust, and who better to trust than the person you learn from?

At networking events, I often hear newer real estate investors, wholesalers, and bird dogs talk about their buyers list and the importance of building it. Yet they never seem to talk about their money list. I've learned that if you have quality deals, buyers will find you. It's the money list needed to get those deals that is the most important. The greatest factor in my ability to become the bank over the years was primarily accomplished through the development of my money list above all else. It's no secret; in fact, it's absurdly simple. I accomplished this by first learning about and using private money and then turning around and teaching this wealth-building strategy to others. It started with my friends and family and later extended to people who attended my writing and speaking events. Today, I have an extremely robust *money list* that's been cultivated over the past thirty-plus years, and it's built largely on trust and track record. Quite simply, doing what you say you're going to do, and staying in communication with your investors, is the only real secret to success.

At this point in the book, I know there are some of you out there who are still too green for that. I get that you can't teach right out the gate and that a network of investors isn't always readily available, especially for those in certain parts of the country. So what do you do if you can't get private money yet?

Hard Money

Private money is pretty hard to beat, but when it's not available, or if a deal is moving past you too quickly, hard money should become your new best friend. As a refresher, hard money refers to loans that are backed by the value of the property, as opposed to loans based on the quality of the borrower (and his or her credit). "But the points! What about the points?!" Yes, I know, before I even get into hard money, there must be readers out there already balking at the idea of this expensive type of capital, but I'm here to debunk that logic. Trust me, when I first heard about the concept of hard money, I contested it with the same exact point. Now that I'm a little older (OK, a lot older) and a little wiser, I understand that I missed the boat by not using it enough.

It wasn't until years later, after being part of a sophisticated real estate investor group in which participants often owned more than one hundred units, that I realized some of the misconceptions I had about hard money were unfounded. Yes, hard money isn't free, I'll admit that, but what it affords you as an investor can certainly lead to profits.

So let's examine how it does this. For one thing, as opposed to HELOCs and personal capital for investments, hard money loans share the risk between you and the hard money lender. Also keep in mind that this risk has already been somewhat mitigated when dealing with an experienced hard money lender, since that lender is also screening the deal before granting the loan. Most of these types of lenders have experience with hundreds of deals (usually focusing on a certain type or a few types of real estate) and have safeguards in place for a reason. They do due diligence on the property, the borrower, and the exit. This last one is important—if they don't believe you can exit with your strategy, they usually won't lend the money. They may also require things like an LLC, a deed in escrow, a certain LTV, a certain amount of reserves, fees, a budget, and the list goes on and on. All of these make sense when learning how much risk they're taking with the deal and even help when underwriting private money deals if you choose to become a lender.

The second thing to consider is that the rate is high—and that can be a good thing! The benefit of the high rate isn't just for the hard money lender—it's beneficial to the investor as well. When I balked at the idea of hard money, what I wasn't looking at was that it was only short-term money, and it was much cheaper than doing a joint venture deal like the one I explained above. It may be better to pay the higher rate and points than to give up half your deal. It also makes an investor move much faster on the deal. I've had many deals with private money lenders in which I would take my time, but if those deals cost me as much as hard money, I think I would have a much different (and much more efficient) mind-set.

Now, I haven't gotten to my most important point yet. I think one of the biggest reasons to utilize hard money is to avoid the lost opportunity cost. Every time you pass on a deal because you don't have the capital, just ask yourself, "How much am I giving up by not acquiring this deal with hard money?" The answer to that question reminds me of when I was an investor-Realtor, selling approximately seventy to seventy-five quality real estate deals a year to my investor friend circle. Instead of buying every deal that came across my desk, I chose to settle for the commission. I passed on all seventy-five of those deals every year because I didn't have the right capital and team in place to buy them on my own. Looking back, if I had used hard money, I believe I could have personally acquired all those deals, and my portfolio today would be massive. I wouldn't have been stepping over dollars to pick up dimes, as the saying goes.

What I've learned from this same circle of friends who now own hundreds of properties themselves is this: They may not use hard money today, but it got them where they wanted to go better and faster. Hard money can really ramp up your real estate buying strategy in a shorter period of time and give you a more robust track record, in turn helping you develop your private money list. It comes back to the great scalability question: How many deals could you do if you had an unlimited supply of money? Well, the answer is that you do have an unlimited supply; you just might not realize it yet.

Making Money on the Draw

There was one other misconception I had before fully understanding hard money, one that I'm going to debunk with a story. One day, I was at an annual private luncheon for an elite group of real estate investors. I was sitting at a table with a friend who has bought and sold easily hundreds of houses. He may have the largest portfolio of SFR properties of anyone I know personally. We had started talking about how he got started in the real estate investing business (prior to becoming a multimillionaire, he worked in a warehouse with my brother-in-law) and that he had done his first thirty-nine deals exclusively with hard money. So my big question was: Hard money is pretty expensive—what would possess you to do thirty-nine deals that way? He said in the beginning, he was new, and the hard money lender taught him a lot about how to buy and shared ideas and resources with him to help him out. When you think about it, it's not so crazy an idea—a more informed borrower is a better borrower, especially for the lender. Over more time and more deals, his hard money lender became easier to work with as they learned to trust each other, even lowering his interest rates and easing his terms. But next he said something that startled me. He said the biggest reason he utilized hard money for these first thirty-nine deals was all the tax-free money he made on the draw. I nearly spit out my water when he said that!

When he said "tax-free money made on the draw," he was referring to the draw schedule—there's that important term yet again! Here's the quick example he gave me: If there was a draw schedule for repairs, the next phase of work was estimated to be $10,000, and he and his seasoned crew got the work done for $6,000, he would be able to put $4,000 in his pocket. Tax-free, too, since this is considered part of the total hard money loan. Aha, I thought, now that makes sense! He went on to explain that this would also help him on the refinance loan that is generally used to "take out" the hard money lender. This is in direct contrast to how the bank usually operates, where often it will allow you to refinance only your money used to acquire and fix up the property. This was just another unique way for him to cash out some of the equity he had created in the property through the renovation.

Now you can start to understand why people will incorporate hard money into their real estate investing strategy. Today, in retrospect, I think one of my biggest regrets was not utilizing more hard money sooner. It would've enabled me to build and grow my portfolio much faster, compared with selling deals to others or waiting to save up my own money to do more deals myself. Thinking small limited my growth. I think this also starts to paint the picture of why many larger real estate investors ended up becoming hard money lenders themselves. Some do it because they already own and manage what they consider to be enough houses. It may seem far away to you now, but how many is enough? Is it 100, 200, 500? Before you decide, try thinking like the bank and lend on a deal or two. You may find the paper side of a deal can be a little bit more interesting and a lot more relaxing.

How to Become a Hard Money Lender

In my experience, and in the experience of my friends, there are two ways that most real estate investors become hard money lenders. One common way is that they have a large portfolio of single-family residences, usually with a commercial blanket on it. Over time, fair market values increase, mortgage debts decrease, and their equity builds. Then they approach their lender for a commercial line of credit. One of my colleagues started his hard money company with a $10 million line of credit against his portfolio and was able to get a great rate on the line and now uses arbitrage and his years of real estate experience to make even more money in the marketplace he knows best. His loans are often 13–18 percent, with three to six points. It's not hard to see that there's plenty of money to be made on this type of spread, and what's his biggest risk? Worst-case scenario, if a deal doesn't work out, he'll take a house back to rehab in his investing area. This is almost a nonissue, since with his volume of properties, he has a rehab crew on standby.

The second way many hard lenders get started is with private equity by starting a hard money real estate fund. This is where you pull private capital, usually from accredited or high–net worth investors, to lend out as hard money loans. This creates a similar form of arbitrage, where the fund managers can charge points and fees to the borrowers and the investors can diversify their risk among many hard money loans. Plus, this way, investors get to limit their liability, since their only risk is their initial investment.

CASE STUDY
TAKING A BANKER TO LUNCH

The biggest game changer for me throughout my real estate investing career has been this concept of utilizing OPM (as a reminder, that's other people's money). I'll never be controlled or held back in my real estate endeavors again because of it. I'm limited only in my ability to find good investments and the relationships I can build with potential investors, which, to me, are limitless. This has also let me and several of my colleagues who believe in this philosophy think bigger...much bigger.

My very good friend and business partner Steve is a person who comes to mind. He was a residential real estate investor like me and really started out as a mentee of mine. A former loan officer, he helped me run a real estate investing networking group for several years. In fact, he was often the emcee at these events and amassed a very large network over that period of time, partly because of it. He also understood traditional banking very well in relation to how he invests. What he did during the real estate crash in 2008 was very simple but brilliant. The financial markets were in complete disarray. Banking was in its darkest hours in decades. He was very uncertain with what to do next in his own investing career. Financing had all but completely dried up with investor loans, which had previously been his specialty. So, unlike the so-called herd who would gripe and grumble, he got proactive and took a banker to lunch.

Lending is constantly changing, and the terms of loans can change dramatically. Certain types of loans can even be created or eradicated over time. For example, when I started, there was an FHA investor loan with 15 percent down. Then that rate went up to 20 percent. Then it went away! Taking a banker to lunch is a simple yet important strategy you can employ to stay on top of these types of changes. Most investors have a mortgage broker they work with or at least know of one. And if they don't, they probably should get to know one.

Steve's lunch with the banker didn't include a "Do you have any money?" or "Where is the money?" conversation because he chose to go into the relationship with an agenda not of what he wanted the bank to do for him but rather of what he could do for the bank. He asked the broker on the other side of the table about the type of loans his bank liked to do right now. And then he took that information a step further. What the banker told him was that, at that time, his bank and many of the banks he knew of were shying away from the riskier, residential loans (e.g., loans to investors, "liar loans," HELOCs, interest-only, adjustable-rate mortgages, no doc loans)—essentially anything other than FHA owner-occupied loans. That was a blow of sorts but something he could understand with the changing regulatory environment. His lunch companion also explained how the banks were now looking at other lines of business, but they still liked commercial loans with good cash flow. They weren't big on construction loans or things like office space either, but they did like apartments because of the solid cash flow.

My friend took this information and ran with it. Instead of sitting on the sidelines and waiting for the market to get better for the type of deals he knew and was used to, he followed what the banker said in a very big way. He began buying run-down properties near a prominent Philadelphia university that had a shortage of off-campus student housing. He would acquire these properties with private money from his investor list, fix them up with private money, and move students in, which gave him amplified cash flow—even more than traditional apartments would have. He would then refinance the newly renovated and rented properties with commercial financing and pay back his private investors with the permanent financing. Then he would turn around and do it all over again. And again. And again.

Today he owns and manages approximately $18 million to $20 million in student housing that he acquired in only a three-to-four-year period, with none of his own money! Best of all, he plans to have it all paid off in less than twelve years total. Needless to say, my friend has done quite well in a real estate market in which others have lost so much. All because of OPM, which helped him realize his dreams when thinking bigger.

What Next?

At the end of the day, all the forms of private capital I described in the previous chapters are just different tools in the tool belt. It's really a matter of using the proper tool for the job at hand. Credit cards have their place with cash management (cash-back rewards, frequent flyer miles, etc.) and temporary expenses (renovation/business supplies) but no longer with hard property purchases, in my opinion, because of high interest rates and cash-advance fees. And I prefer to utilize HELOCs on all my properties to work my equity to the maximum amount by leveraging my assets through debt while creating a healthy return in a diversified portfolio. The investments in this case have usually been short-term private money loans for fellow rehabbers and, later on, liquid institutional notes. I choose these two collateral-backed investments because of the agility short-term loans give me with their time frame or the liquidity that notes will end up giving me with their ability to sell online, sometimes nearly instantly. Plus these low-maintenance notes can be borrowed against, as well, but I don't want to get ahead of myself.

As for private and hard money, I continued to use both for acquisitions of all types but really stuck to private money, since it was easily available. I learned that my standing as a borrower and lender was growing fast, leading me to more ventures into raising larger amounts of money. I still use private money today, only I'm raising equity instead of debt (more on that later). My real estate investing journey doesn't end here; in fact, it's only just beginning. Now that I have access to potentially limitless money and my deal flow is at capacity, probably the result of my reputation more than anything, I continue on into nearly a decade of deal after deal, chasing everything that comes my way. What's interesting now is to see that I was using notes all along, but unlike before, I was ready to really get creative with them and buy some serious real estate!

CHAPTER 5
TAKEAWAYS

Venturing into the world of hard/private money. Discovering the power of OPM (other people's money) is impossible to exaggerate. Game changer of all game changers.

The value of your cell phone (hint: the money's in your contact list). A common fallacy is that you don't have access to private money, but private money can come from anywhere and anyone. It's all about whom you know and how reputable you are to them.

A warning about partnerships. Combining forces and capital can be a great way to move faster. It can also be clumsy, inefficient, and aggravating.

The car wash deal. You never know where you'll find a motivated seller.

Why private money can beat a joint venture. Capital is worth only interest and points (paid as a return), not equity.

How to protect your private money deal. Document your deal, know the value of the property, get insured, know your property, know the borrower's track record, and do a title search (borrower) and get title insurance (borrower and lender).

IRA funds can be a great source of private money. As a fund-raiser, this source of capital can almost become your private bank.

Hard money. It's worth the points. Or at least it can be. It comes with less risk, and it's cheaper than the lost opportunity cost. Plus you can make tax-free money on the draw.

Becoming a hard money lender. Use your real estate equity or private equity to start a hard money fund.

Steve's story: Take a banker to lunch and build an empire. This may be one of the most important stories in this book. What Steve did was brilliant because he turned conventional thinking on its head and made millions from it. He asked what the bank wanted, they told, and he did it! Absurdly simple but genius.

CHAPTER 6

Other Ways Notes and Creative Financing Can Fund or Create Deals

I didn't have much of a long-term plan. I was doing deals that seemed to be coming at me day to day. Maybe it wasn't just a plan I was missing but also a lack of knowing myself— my strengths as an investor, what field of real estate I truly enjoyed, or even my personal limits with owning residential property. The only thing I knew was that I wanted to keep learning because that seemed like the only way I could get to those answers. So I became a sponge.

At this point in my career, I was more or less "retired" from my contracting business after my injury, so I had plenty of time on my hands. And although I was starting to obtain a decent-sized portfolio, I also had a family to feed, so I had to start doing some serious deals. I went to every DIG class available and every networking meeting that would have me, and I read constantly. I saw all the gurus: the good, the bad, and the ugly. There's a circuit of sorts with most people of note passing through the major cities, and since I was attending every Philadelphia-area DIG meeting, some South Jersey and Delaware REIAs, as well as many of their subgroups (along with the occasional NYC or Baltimore meeting), I started to see everyone and everything. It helped in many ways because the more I attended, the better I got at spotting the phonies, the inexperienced, or the just plain bad investments. Plus it helped me later in more ways than one.

I eventually formed my own group called RING (Real Estate Investors Networking Group) that started out in the Philadelphia region but, over the course of many years, grew to six different cities across five different states. As the cofounder and manager of that intimate group, I had to interview many speakers, and with all my networking group experience, I could spot a valuable educator (and the not-so-valuable ones) from a mile away. Attending all these meetings also helped me later when I became a speaker myself and someone who would have to corral a room of investors for a private money project. When I got into institutional notes, I even became an educator of sorts in the space, with my own course on the note business. The main reason I did this, outside my desire to teach, was really just to explain the second lien note space! It was such a small market back then that we literally had to teach people of its existence. But I digress.

Seeing these speakers week after week, presenting new investment opportunities and strategies, and connecting with fellow investors all following different paths led me through a couple of different industries. I had dabbled in everything from hard real estate to day-trading options and briefly sold life insurance and annuities. Out of RING, I even became a part owner of a title company. I wasn't working in the operations or general day-to-day, but I drove plenty of business there, including my own. The more volume I would drive there quarterly, the more I would make as a partner.

Also with my large network, I found it advantageous to start a property management company, with which I found my niche in working exclusively with local investors. The usual brokerage/property manager compensation works on roughly a 50/50 split (which can be somewhat negotiable), but my situation was a little different and, in my opinion, much more worthwhile.

I was 100 percent commission at my real estate brokerage, having to pay only a $1,500 flat fee per month to operate as a Realtor and a property manager. So instead of having to split every fee I received for my work or every residual payment, I would pay my brokerage its flat fee, and in exchange, I would be able to operate legally as a property manager, and it would handle all the paperwork, accounting, etc. I also worked only with investors who had properties in the same areas that I operated in, so checking in on these places when necessary was really just a few minutes' drive while managing my own portfolio. If I showed a place to a potential tenant and he or she was accepted,

I would make a quick $1,000 as my fee and a small percentage of the rent every month. It quickly became a good source of additional income as well as residual income. And since my clientele was almost exclusively investors who purchased the same types of properties in the same areas, these weren't emotional purchases like a first-time home buyer looking to start a family. These folks knew what they wanted and where they wanted it, and I did too.

As these endeavors started to come together and I had built a trusted group of investor buyers, I got lucky when I went to, you'll never guess, my local real estate networking group! At this particular meeting, I saw a man named Robert Allen. He was a bit of the old guard, an intellectual who ran in similar circles with the likes of Robert Kiyosaki and Jack Canfield. He had written a book called *Multiple Streams of Income* and spoken in depth about the revolutionary topic, specifically in relation to cash flow and expense management. What particularly stuck out for me was the simplicity of this concept: Evaluate all your profit centers and expenses, then try to figure out how to maximize these centers and profit from where you would usually spend money.

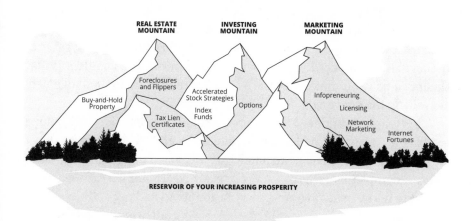

Robert Allen's Mountain Range of Financial Freedom. Allen, Robert G. *Multiple Streams of Income: How to Generate a Lifetime of Unlimited Wealth.* Wiley, 2013. Page 43.

I bought his book that night. Almost immediately, I found it to be an invaluable read, and I highly suggest it to every investor, new and old. Even if you've read the book in the past, it's a good idea to revisit it, with Allen's material and strategy getting only richer with more knowledge and experience. What he was saying got me thinking: The banks don't have one profit center; they have a multitude, just within the concepts of interchange, fees, and net interest margin alone. So why not do the same? What were my profit centers, and how could I maximize them to the fullest? I had to figure out how I could apply Allen's theories to what I did. I started with the profit centers of the properties in my portfolio.

Highest and Best Use of Your Property

One of the best things Allen's book did for me was trigger the idea of "the highest and best use" of a property. "Highest and best use" is a theory around the idea of maximum productivity and was discovered by the (in)famous economist Irving Fisher. I say *infamous* because many of Fisher's theories have been either debunked or forgotten over those of his contemporaries like John Maynard Keyes (of "Keynesian economics"), especially after he was reported as saying the stock market had reached "what looks like a permanently high plateau" just days prior to the 1929 crash. I had learned of Fisher and his concept when I took my brokerage courses many years before but only the general theory. Then Robert Allen's book reminded me of how I could put that theory to use and maximize the assets I already had instead of solely searching for new deals.

This "highest and best use of your property" concept really helped me take a step back and look at my portfolio and the properties that I was looking to purchase with a new pair of eyes. There are many ways you could implement this concept. For example, I bought a two-bedroom property in my usual area of expertise for about $26,000. I finished the attic and ran heat up to the third floor, essentially turning a two-bedroom property into a four-bedroom home, making $1,150 a month (versus $650 if it were a two-bedroom) and having it appraised soon after for about $80,000. The examples go on and on. I've turned first-floor kitchens into bedrooms (while eliminating dining rooms), turned small six-units into very large three-units, turned large one-bedrooms into smaller two-bedrooms, made an enclosed front porch into a bedroom by adding heat and electric—you name it, I've done it.

Then I started thinking about the space surrounding my properties. This is where the theory really came in handy, and that was by dropping prefab garages, renting each separately. In my eventual portfolio of forty-plus properties, I ended up with an additional eleven garages. On one of my duplexes alone, I built a four-bay garage in the spacious backyard area that now generates an additional $660 a month in rent. Plus garages can be much easier to manage than tenant-occupied residences. I've found my garage renters to be more long-term, and they rarely call for anything to be repaired (probably since it's in use for less time than an actual residence). This was all fruitful, but it was generating only one stream of income rather than multiple streams. So I started to think about how my deal existed and came to be and realized it was much bigger than just the property itself.

The Life Cycle of a Deal

Every deal exists within a cycle, from purchase to exit. You market for a deal (or it finds you), and then there's due diligence on the deal itself, making the offer on it, purchasing, renovating (usually), and exiting the deal—either renting or selling. After studying Allen's book, I discovered that by only finding my deals and making money on the flip or buy-and-hold cash flow, I was losing out on so many other revenue streams . I decided I would devise a system for every deal that came my way based on my expertise and network as an investor-Realtor, along with aspects of my newfound endeavors in my title company and property management business. Most of the deals would be cookie-cutter, with the same school district, same type of property, same rent range, etc. I was already helping investors with their deals in these areas, either as a Realtor, title company owner, or property manager, but now I was shopping deals to them and capitalizing on them every step of the way. Doesn't that sound like a lot? Well, in some ways it was, but these were processes and tasks I was doing already—now I was simply monetizing all of them to their maximum potential. On top of that, any deal that didn't fit the mold for my investors, I would purchase myself and run it through my title company, my real estate brokerage, and my property management company. I would then be paid on the back end from either the rent/appreciation or the sale of the house. Now, I admit that *does* sound like a lot and is probably best explained with an example.

RENT/
APPRECIATION

PURCHASE
THE HOUSE

REAL ESTATE
BROKERAGE

TITLE
COMPANY

PROPERTY
MANAGEMENT
COMPANY

SALE OF
THE HOUSE

How a traditional real estate deal would give the author multiple streams of income. Based on a graphic created by Ryan Krail of Lightmark Media, December 4, 2017.

Real Estate Deal vs. a Maximized Real Estate Deal

Earlier, I used an example of a deal in which my cousin provided private money. I proposed two scenarios: one where I chose to joint-venture with him and one where I chose not to joint-venture with him. After running through the two scenarios, I knew it would be more work and less profitable for me overall if I chose to joint-venture. I know he's my cousin and all, and I do love him, but I don't love him that much! When I look back on the deal with all my knowledge from Robert Allen, I realize with that property specifically, I was looking only at how I maximized the financing to acquire and fix up this deal—but it didn't stop there.

Most rehabbers would have fixed this place up and sold it. The cost to acquire the home plus the fix-up totaled approximately $200,000, and the place appraised at $320,000. If I'd sold it upon completion, I would've paid selling costs of 7.25 percent ($23,200), which consisted of Realtor fees of 6 percent ($19,200) plus a transfer tax of 1.25 percent ($4,000). In this scenario, my profit would also have been taxed as ordinary income, which was particularly troublesome for me, since it would have put my tax rate into a higher bracket for that year. Meaning my tax on the short-term capital gain would have been upward of 30 percent, or at least $29,280, and I would have netted only $68,320.

But, and this is a big but, if I'd held the property for at least one year and a day, my tax would have been considered a long-term capital gain of approximately 15 percent–plus, or at least $14,640. My tax bill would have been much less, and I could have netted $82,960 total ($14,640 more). So that's what I did, renting it to a doctor who was doing her residency in Philadelphia. With market rent putting her monthly payment at $1,750, my cash flow still wasn't great. I had to think of another way to improve it. And a familiar note concept was what got me there.

Another Way to Use HELOCs

Not long after I rented the property to the doctor, I applied for a line of credit (HELOC) against the property for approximately $67,000. My current first mortgage payment was $1,450/month, which I paid with my tenant's $1,750/month rent. What I did next was to take the $67,000 HELOC money at 4 percent interest only and use that money to do a private money deal at 15–18 percent. This arbitrage spread of 11–14 percent let me juice the cash flow generating from this property. After all, the rate of return of the equity in this property was zero percent. If I hadn't done that, the profits for my rehab project would've been trapped in the property's equity. Now my cash flow went from $300 a month to $1,081 a month. The beauty of the private money deal is that they're short-term, high-yield, and secured to hard real estate. It was a perfect match for my investing goals. Now I was able to maximize cash flow and use of my equity and reduce capital gains, all to help me build more wealth and net worth sooner.

The doctor ended up staying in the property for a year and then moved on because she'd completed her residency. I now had to make the decision to either sell or keep the property again. This time, market values had fallen a little. I didn't like the idea of doing maintenance, so I sold the property on a lease option—which happens when the property owner and tenant agree that the renter has the option of purchasing the property at the end of the rental period—to a nice couple with two kids. The husband was principal of a local school. They stayed a few years and then exercised their right to buy the property. This was great for me because I didn't have to pay any Realtor fees to sell, and now I had a long-term capital gain instead of a short-term one.

Lease Options

I wasn't quite done maximizing this asset to its full potential yet. Around this time, in a sea of REIA meetings, I came across a very talented writer and speaker named Wendy Patton. Being both a broker and builder, she'd homed in on the strategy of lease options and built a mini empire around it, in both the United States and the United Kingdom. In fact, she wrote the book on lease options. No, literally, she wrote *Investing in Real Estate with Lease Options and "Subject-To" Deals: Powerful Strategies for Getting More When You Sell, and Paying Less When You Buy*, which is probably the most definitive book out there on the subject. Needless to say, Wendy is the Queen of Lease Options. Now, many people who follow Wendy's strategy are starting with either no- or low-money-down deals and creating a business out of the lease options or subject-to (which I'll get into more in the next chapter) properties. My situation was a little different. I already had the property in my possession, and the lease option let me obtain a larger deposit and a higher rent, and it got me out of the maintenance business (since the occupant was becoming an owner rather than simply a renter).

Here's how my lease option worked: We had a two-year lease option in place that started January 1, 2008, and included a nonrefundable option deposit (not the same as a security deposit) for $5,800. I was receiving top-of-the-market rent for $1,750/month, with a rent credit of $200/month, and a seller assist of 3 percent of the sales price. This was a huge win for me, the seller, as I didn't have to pay a Realtor for finding the tenant and I had no property management fees nor a real estate commission of 6 percent ($19,200 on $320,000) on the sale. It also got me out of the repair business, since the tenant/buyer agreed to be responsible for all repairs. I made sure to provide a home warranty to make the tenant/buyer feel more comfortable in this responsibility, without his or her having any threat of a major repair. Besides, the home in this case had gone through a complete renovation a short time earlier.

Whenever I do a lease option with a tenant, I use two documents: a regular Association of Realtors residential (plain language) lease and a separate option to purchase agreement. If and when the tenants send me a written request that exercises their option to purchase, I'll then draw up an agreement of sale to purchase the property. Technically these residents are tenants *until* they exercise the option to purchase the home. My risk here is limited because I have received a large deposit that's nonrefundable, a good selling price, a quality monthly rental payment stream, and no repairs to worry about. You can see why it's easier to assist with the purchase if I don't have to pay the Realtor's fee for selling the property.

But it's not all about me. This is a big win for the tenant/buyer as well because he or she can move into his or her dream home now—in mint condition, with a home warranty—and put all the deposit/down payment toward closing costs, along with the $200-a-month credit for two years ($4,800 plus $5,800) plus the 3 percent assist ($9,600), for a total credit of $20,000. Potential buyers strapped for cash commonly utilize capital from their 401(k) or, if it's around tax time, their tax return, and you can see how easy it becomes for them to purchase this home.

All right, so this is where the deal ends. Right? Well, not exactly. It's where the deal ends for the time being. The last part of the cycle on most deals is the exit, and we didn't quite get there yet. There are still a few years that must go by until the buyer/tenant is ready to purchase, around the same exact time that I discover the power of seller-financed notes. This is when I figured out a way to, again, increase my revenue on this very property, even after I sell it. But let's not jump the gun; I still have a few more years of hard real estate to get creative with, and in the meantime, I have a lease option that is netting me $3,600/year ($1,750 in rent minus my $1,450 mortgage payment, times twelve), and I collected $5,800 in a nonrefundable option deposit.

CHAPTER 6
TAKEAWAYS

Learn as much as you can. Becoming a sponge at every REIA, reading every real estate book, and connecting with others put me in touch with strategies I would never have imagined.

Robert Allen's insight. Get the "highest and best use of your property." In other words, maximize your deal with as many revenue streams as possible.

Putting lease options to work...a win-win solution. Lease options can be a great way to maximize certain deals, and they provide a way to buy a home for some homeowners who are locked out of conventional financing.

CHAPTER 7

Taking Over a Note (and a Property) via Subject-To Investing

Saying I've met a lot of investors over the years would be an understatement. Traveling the country and regularly attending local networking meetings, I sometimes feel as if I've met them all! But time and again, I'm introduced to new people with a new story that I haven't heard or a new twist on an investment. Yet at the end of the day, it always comes down to the numbers game. So it may not come as a surprise to hear that only a handful of people I meet are super successful. It also may not come as a surprise that the majority of people I meet are newbies. Whenever I meet new real estate investors, they're looking for one of two things that an investor needs to be successful: the money or the deal. It was only after I had capital and consistent deal flow that I stumbled on a way that will find you both. Remember Wendy Patton? I mostly focused on the "lease option" part of her career, but there is another strategy, which is even mentioned in the subtitle of her book, that's just as important, and that's subject-to investing.

What Is Subject-To Real Estate?

When someone purchases a house subject-to, that's really shorthand for purchasing a home subject to the existing mortgage. There are many types of subject-to clauses one can put into a contract when buying a home, including *subject to* attorney review, *subject to* buyer's inspection, and *subject to* finding a quality resident (with a lease option, for instance). In the realm of real estate investing tools, the subject-to many refer to (including myself) is when distressed homeowners need to exit their property and an investor is willing to buy into their mortgage with little or no money. Hold on—you may not have gotten that. I said a seller is essentially willing to give away his or her property (or sell it for a song), and the buyer doesn't necessarily need any financing. That's right. But hey, it's not the lottery. There are a few things that have to happen for a subject-to deal to make sense.

Why Would a Seller Be Willing to Sell Subject-To?

This was probably the toughest thing for me to understand when I first heard about this strategy. Why wouldn't sellers just sell the home? Why would they give up their equity or everything they've put into the property thus far? Why would they jeopardize their credit? Once I started to really connect with distressed sellers, I soon discovered the *why*. Unfortunately, bad things happen to good people, and sometimes they get themselves into tough situations or they just plain run out of time.

The first subject-to deal I ever encountered didn't involve my acquiring any property. I was more of a sideline player, practicing as a real estate agent in the deal, who saw an opportunity for one of my investor-buyer friends who was in my inner circle.

The House in Question

From the outside, Flora Lane was a three-bedroom/one-bathroom property in a nice family neighborhood and quality school district that I was going to list in my area of expertise. The owner wanted to retire to his vacation home in another state. On visiting the property, I realized pretty fast that this place was in no condition to list. Even in as-is condition with a For Sale by Owner sign, I knew this thing wouldn't move. The owner had acquired quite a few items over the decade he'd lived there. Calling it a handyman special in the ad would have been, well, a compliment. He was also behind on a payment or two and about to be behind on another. Plus, considering he'd have to pay a combined Realtor commission and transfer tax of 7–8 percent at the sale, it left him with few options. I didn't want to leave the owner hanging, though, so I took the deal to my friend Tom. Tom was a general contractor who specialized in fix-and-flips. Originally, Tom was going to attempt to purchase the home strictly as a short sale, but he knew it would be a struggle to come up with the financing. He shared the mind-set of many investors', where he wasn't exactly excited about paying the going rate of 15–18 percent for hard money plus points and fees. Luckily, I remembered the teachings of Wendy and some other investor friends over the years who had specialized in the strategy of subject-to.

Walking into a Note: The Advantages of Subject-To for the Buyer

After putting the owner and Tom in touch, my friend was able to acquire this house, worth $145,000, subject to the mortgage. All with zero out of pocket! Plus walking into a homeowner-friendly mortgage rate of 7 percent that'd been paid on for quite a few years was much more favorable than starting new with a hard money loan (and another mortgage if he were to refinance). As soon as Tom was given the deed, he hired cleaning crews to clear out the property and ended up completing about $28,000 of renovations. Because of the money he had to put into the renovations, Tom's choice to do a subject-to made much more sense, since he could acquire the deed from the original owner (as opposed to a lease option, where that wouldn't be the case).

In exchange for the property, Tom brought the loan current and was able to pick up the loan payments in a favorable spot of the amortization schedule (where the Principle and Interest payment is more P than I). He got all the tax advantages of being an owner, as well as low closing costs (similar to a cash deal with no lender points and fees, appraisals, etc.). He was also able to do a quick closing (although he still needed title insurance) and was able to receive a favorable interest rate (since it was an owner-occupied loan at origination). He didn't need to qualify for a newly originated mortgage, and it didn't even show on his credit. So he had no personal liability on the debt because the mortgage was still technically in the previous owner's name. The beauty of it all was that by acquiring this property subject-to, he was afforded long-term financing without ever talking to a bank. After completing renovations, Tom was able to sell the house for a profit of about $195,000, with a final sale price of $225,000.

Walking Away from a Note: Advantages for the Seller

So what did the seller get out of all of this? Well, being motivated to leave and retire in another state, the previous owner could walk away from his house (and everything in it) to retire immediately thanks to Tom. The previous owner didn't have to wait for the house to sell on the market. He also didn't have to clean it out or fix a thing. Oh, and he didn't need a home inspection, a certificate of occupancy, or a termite report either. He simply took what belongings he wanted and left Tom to deal with the rest. In fact, he didn't even pay any Realtor fees or normal closing costs because I agreed to let him take it off the market, since Tom would let me list the newly renovated house. Sometimes subject-to sellers have the fear of a subject-to buyer not making payments on their behalf, but in this case, both Tom and the seller had access online to see whether the loan payments were being made. The contractor also had a history of doing these types of renovation deals in the past, and on top of that, the seller felt he was at an age when he may never need his credit to buy another place in the future anyway. Regardless, Tom saved him from harming his credit and a possible foreclosure by reinstating the loan and continuing to make payments.

The Pitfalls of Subject-To

By now, you may be thinking, What's the catch? And you're right, this isn't an entirely risk-free strategy. There are some things to be cautious of. Remember what I said about having the right tool for the right job? I referenced title insurance when Tom was purchasing a subject-to deal because one of the major risks is that there could be existing liens on the property. If that were the case, subject-to might not make sense. Luckily, in the example I presented above, this wasn't an issue, but it pays to be sure by pulling title and utilizing a good real estate attorney in your state, especially the first time around. But that's not the only thing to keep in mind. Anytime I mention subject-to, there's always a Nervous Nellie who objects with the statement "What about the due-on-sale clause?"

The Due-on-Sale Clause

There's no doubt that the due-on-sale clause could squander your deal, but I'm here to tell you the likelihood of that happening. For those of you unfamiliar or who haven't taken a good look at your mortgage docs recently (because this clause is in most), this is a clause in the original loan documents of the seller saying, in essence, that if the title is transferred or changes hands, the bank has the right to "call the loan" due and in full. Keep in mind, it says the "right" to call the loan, so the real question is, How often does that happen?

As someone who has done hundreds, if not thousands, of sub-ject-to deals over the years, largely from foreclosing from the junior lien position (more on that later), I can recall only one time when a bank would not allow us to reinstate a first mortgage, thus calling the mortgage due. And this was because it knew the borrower was deceased.

In another instance, I had a friend who took over a local home sub-ject-to and turned it into a rental property. The mortgage company sold the loan to a third party, which then called the loan due, since the third party noticed it had transferred hands and there was equity available in the home. In this case, my friend simply refinanced the property and paid the lender off. So she was still able to make it work. If you're considering investing with subject-to, it's always good to be aware of this possibility and have reserves or access to cash if this situation should occur. It's also important to remember that the lender would have to take you all the way to foreclosure for you to really lose out, and that's usually plenty of time to sell or refinance the property. The foreclosure timelines vary from state to state. In Pennsylvania, it usually takes about a year to foreclose, and in Tom's case (if that were to happen), he had renovated and sold the property much sooner than that. As the investor, though, even if all these worst-case scenarios happened, the most you'd lose is maybe renovation costs. The foreclo-sure wouldn't affect your credit, and you most likely had little money in the deal to begin with.

Insurance

Another issue may be determining who should insure the property and whether a change in the insurance policy would trigger the bank to exercise the due-on-sale clause. The owner of the property should own the policy. Also, leaving the seller's policy intact and just getting another one for the new buyer, thus having two policies on the property at the same time, is probably not a good idea, since you might have a situation in which both insurance companies would be trying to deny a claim if one were to occur. Usually the best and easiest thing to do is to have all parties named as insured or additional insured on the one policy, including previous and current owners.

Outside those few things, the only other potential issue you could run into is needing a seller's signature down the road. In my first example, Tom cleaned out the property and fixed it all up. I then went on to sell the newly renovated property to a nice family. In fact, I got to make an even larger commission selling a more valuable property than I would have if I had sold the property in as-is condition for the original seller (so take note, all of you Realtors, trying to maximize your deals). But since the seller moved out of state, he couldn't personally sign on the account. Fortunately, my friend Tom was smart enough to get limited power of attorney from the seller and the seller's authorization to speak on the account on his behalf, which gave him the ability to sign documents regarding the property. This was a huge plus for Tom once he sold the property, since he received a check for a few thousand dollars that was put into escrow (for taxes and insurance payments) when the owner took out the original mortgage.

With so many advantages for the buyer and seller of a subject-to deal, this creative note strategy can make for a handy tool in an investor's tool belt. Be that as it may, it's not a tool that works for every job or can be applied anywhere. I often meet newbies with little to no access to capital who think subject-to is their salvation. Those whom I've encountered who've had great success with it see it as merely one option of many to present to a distressed seller. It must fit the criteria, and if it doesn't, that's OK because there are more note strategies that can help investors. In fact, in the next deal that I'm about to show you, I encountered a new strategy that may be a perfect fit.

CHAPTER 7
TAKEAWAYS

Buying a property subject-to. If you can't get a mortgage, walk into one.

Subject-tos can be a win-win. Both buyers and sellers can benefit from this strategy.

The pitfalls of subject-to. Existing liens, the due-on-sale clause, and trouble with insurance.

CHAPTER 8
Use Notes through Owner Financing

I first heard the term owner financing from a Realtor who worked at my very first brokerage in the late 1980s. He was the creative guy whom I shadowed but clearly should have shadowed more, since I didn't implement the strategy of helping owners finance their own home upon purchase. He was always talking about "owner financing," but he was also talking about all these other creative strategies, so I guess that idea got shoved under the rug. Then I joined DIG and saw Jimmy Napier speak about "seller financing" (same thing as owner financing, just a more investor-friendly term), in which an investor buys a privately created note. These notes are usually bought and sold at a discount and have conservative underwriting or terms. Many borrowers in these types of notes may not have met the requirements expected by a bank (whether those are credit, income, etc.), hence the reason someone created a note privately with them.

The people who tend to buy these notes are generally real estate investors looking for a passive return that's comparable to SFR cash flow without having to deal with the tenants, maintenance, or most hassles that come along with hard property. To get these notes, buyers can find individual-seller-financed note sellers, market for these notes, and even try to reach out directly to the seller-financed note owners, who may be listed in the county courthouse records. Or, in an effort to save time, there are also brokers who've already done the hard work for you and offer these notes for sale often through a trade desk. Of course, this convenience comes at a cost but can still be a viable source of seller-financed notes. These trade desks may even buy seller-financed notes from individuals and, in turn, sell them through their platform. Many of the experts and speakers in the space buy and broker these types of notes in a similar fashion.

So I heard this pretty interesting, relatively passive strategy to invest in real estate without all the hassles of property ownership and did nothing with it. Years later, I heard about it again from a very talented seller-financing specialist known as Donna Bauer. She brought this whole other side of the real estate industry, the note business, to my attention yet again. I didn't realize there was an entire marketplace for these types of notes, with buyers and sellers all over the country, until I heard her speak. I think part of this had to do with my location. In judicial states, like Pennsylvania, it can be legally cumbersome to foreclose, but deed-of-trust states (like Texas and Florida) are more lender friendly. So that's part of the reason that in Texas, for example, you'll see notes for sale in the newspaper, just as you'd see a house for sale.

At this point, I was an active real estate investor interested in hard property. I wasn't fed up with all the hassles of owning or managing SFRs—I loved it! I also wasn't all that interested in a passive investment vehicle when I could actively make a profit. But after hearing Jimmy, Donna, and a few others talk about seller financing, I tried to distill the strategy to fit my situation.

I met an accountant in my RING networking group who had a really large "We Buy Houses" company. He was one of the people who got me thinking of the "tools in the tool belt" way of operating when a deal came my way. When I asked him about owner financing, he said he loved the strategy and had used it plenty of times. What he would do when a deal came his way was make three to five offers, all of which would work for him. Some involved owner financing, others subject-to, and still others even lease options if they were applicable. Then he would narrow down the options with sellers by asking them an array of questions, like:

- "Where are you going when you sell this?"
- "What are your plans with the proceeds? Are you living off it? Is it for retirement? Are you buying another house?"
- "Would you be interested in holding paper?"

Multiple Offers

It may sound simple on paper, but you'd be shocked at how few investors ask questions and listen to their motivated sellers. I know because I've been guilty of it myself. It wasn't until this idea of making multiple offers that I really came to understand that I would never know what the seller's true needs or hot buttons were unless I asked. Sure, I can make a low cash offer like anyone else, but perhaps I can make different offers with flexible variations of financing and let the seller pick the situation that's best for them. Meanwhile, all the offer structures would already fit my needs and may even differentiate me from any other "We Buy Houses" bidders.

A Brief Example

So let's say motivated sellers—senior citizens, for instance—call in on my "We Buy Houses—Any Situation/Any Condition" ad and want to sell their house to move closer to their children, who were out of state, a pretty common occurrence. Like many seniors, they have lived in their home for forty-plus years, the property is paid off, there is some deferred maintenance, and there are some things in the home that are functionally obsolete, but it still makes for a good rental property. Let's also say they'd accumulated a lot of stuff in the home over the years. They tell me they intend to sell and move in with their son in California. This would be the perfect multiple-offer situation.

At the time, in my area of expertise, a three-bedroom/two-bathroom house may have sold for $125,000 in pristine condition. This house may also need average renovations totaling $25,000. So they're probably asking an unrealistic $115,000 for it. They're probably not willing to give me a thirty-year mortgage on this property, but in this case, I might make my offer something like this: $110,000 for ten years at 5 percent interest, amortized over thirty years. Then after the ten years is up, I can either refinance or sell the property to pay them back the remaining balance on the loan. I could also make it a shorter term (like five years), but in that case, I would try to go to interest-only to lower my monthly payments. I would then show them these options and how they would've compared with their selling and putting the proceeds in the bank. Since I won't need a new mortgage from the bank, this will also save me money in bank closing fees. After I explain all of this, I go, "Think about it, but here's what else we could do."

My second offer might be $90,000, with a $25,000 seller-second mortgage carried over five years that's interest only. This allows me money to fix it up and still get a first mortgage on the property, either through a traditional bank or with private money. After which, I again say, "Think about it, but here's another option."

My third offer might be $75,000—all cash, as is, and a quick close. Depending on how truly motivated they are to leave, this might be the right fit. Other variations of these offers may come up in our conversation, but either way, I'm giving them options.

Seller Seconds

If you noticed above, my first two options involved owner financing through what is known as a seller-carry note, or a seller-second mortgage. This is one of my favorite owner-financing strategies when selling my rental properties because, to put it simply, I can still cash-flow off a property after I sell it and without owning it. Yes, you read that correctly. And for the buyer, a seller second can also be used to cover down payments, closing costs, and even repair credits. So it really can be a win-win scenario for both the buyer and the seller.

I learned a little later in my career that in commercial real estate, second mortgages held by a seller are very common, since many commercial loans become portfolio loans that are often held by local banks. If local banks do a first mortgage for 70–80 percent of value, they usually feel pretty good about it, since they have a strong equity position in the property. They tend to weigh the asset more than the borrower. This is especially true with assets like apartment complexes that are greater than one hundred units, for which they may allow a nonrecourse first mortgage (i.e., 70 percent loan-to-value or lower). If the remaining money down and closing costs come from the buyer, the seller, or private equity, for that matter, it's usually perfectly acceptable to the lender. In the world of residential, it's much different. Many residential lenders, especially with owner-occupied loans, want to verify where the borrower's down payment and closing funds are coming from, as they put a lot more weight into the borrower and not just the property. But with residential rentals, the seller second is a very valuable tool whether you're buying or selling. I first learned this for myself when selling one of my mother's investment properties.

245 Lexington

In the mid-'90s, I helped my mother buy a SFR investment property for $26,500. It was one of three properties she'd purchased using her small pool of retirement money she pulled out of the stock market. The cash flow from the properties had helped supplement her retirement income. She owned the property for about ten years, but with more and more maintenance for us becoming necessary (especially since I was managing so many other properties) and the signs of a high market, we decided to sell. In the time since she'd purchased the home, the house had more than doubled in value, nearing $70,000. Coincidentally, at the same time, my friend and future partner in the note business, Bob, whom I met at RING, was looking to purchase some low-cost rentals with his LLC.

Most investors like Bob are usually buying a property in an entity, meaning they're using commercial financing or simply adding another property to their commercial blanket. With commercial financing, the lower loan-to-value of a first mortgage they apply for will have more favorable terms, as opposed to an owner-occupied residential loan. Because we were financing part of the home cost through our seller second, he received a better rate on his senior lien. Commercial lenders are usually OK with creative financing like this, since their position is well protected. Because of this, we didn't have to stress out as much about low appraisals or stricter loan-to-value requirements being imposed, since we could just readjust the second lien loan amount if necessary. Being an investor himself, Bob was the perfect buyer for a scenario like this, since he understands creative financing and the rental space and has access to local resources to fix up properties and manage tenants. To provide incentive and help my friend, I structured the deal as a no-money-down purchase with a seller-assist and seller-carry second mortgage. Here were the terms of the purchase:

Purchase price: $26,500

Sales price: $70,000

Seller-second mortgage: $14,000 interest only for five years at 10 percent

Monthly payment: $116.67

Two-point (i.e., 2 percent of the loan amount) prepayment penalty

Profit from the sale: $43,500

Profit from the note: $7,000

Total profit: $50,500

It's easy to see from the above scenario that my mother did very well in this deal. Not only did she profit from the appreciation when selling the property (which was cash-flowing around $400/month the entire time she owned it), but she was also able to cash-flow for five years after selling it without any maintenance, tenants, township inspections, or headaches. Plus within the transaction itself, she was able to save the 6 percent Realtor commission because I was able to do the paperwork privately and run it through my title company. Bob eventually refinanced at maturity and paid us off in full. Nothing's better than getting the best price for the property, fewer fees from the bank, and more overall yield for everyone involved.

The Lease Option Returns

It wasn't long after 245 Lexington that I figured I could add this as a tool in the tool belt for other deals of my own. Remember the property from the lease option story in Chapter 6? Well, it wasn't long after this last deal that the lease option on that property was about to hit maturity and the owner was looking to purchase the property. The unique situation with the lease option there was that with the larger price tag for the home because of the location, size, and renovations I'd completed, there came a larger capital gain. So with a sizable capital gain of $120,000, I knew if I sold right away, the tax would have been around $30,000 out of pocket. By holding it a year and a day (at a minimum), the gain dropped to $15,000, since it was now considered a long-term capital gain. The lease option enabled me that freedom, but now it was a few years later and time for the tenant to exercise her option to buy, but there were two issues.

MORTGAGE

THIS MORTGAGE made the _30th_ day of October, 2009, between

Mortgagor(s),

and Mortgagee(s),

WITNESSETH:

Mortgagor has executed and delivered to Mortgagee a Promissory Note ("Note") bearing the same date as this mortgage, wherein Mortgagor promise to pay to Mortgagee the principal sum of **EIGHTEEN THOUSAND DOLLARS and 00/100 ($18,000.00)** lawful money of the United States of America, advanced or to be advanced by Mortgagee to Mortgagors, to be paid in the manner and according to the terms and conditions specified in the Note, all of the terms of which are incorporated herein by reference, due on or before **October 9, 2014.**

NOW, THEREFORE, in consideration of the indebtedness, and as security for payment to Mortgagee of the principal and all other sums provided for in the Note and in this Mortgage, according to their respective terms and conditions, and for performance of the agreements, conditions, covenants, provisions and stipulations contained in this Mortgage and in the Note, Mortgagor have granted, conveyed bargained, sold, alienated, enfeoffed, released, confirmed and mortgaged, and by these presents do hereby grant, convey, bargain, sell, alien, enfeoff, release, confirm and mortgage unto Mortgagees all that certain real estate located at:

as more fully described in Exhibit "A" attached hereto and made a part hereof.

TOGETHER WITH all of Mortgagors' right, title and interest now owned or hereafter acquired in:

(1) all buildings and improvements erected or hereafter erected thereon; and

A copy of the author's seller-second mortgage.

The first problem was the market was not what it used to be. Nearing the time of the crash and an overall slump in that local area, I had to figure out a way to still maximize my profit on this deal. On top of that, my tenant-buyer had a good income but didn't have enough money to make the full purchase. So once again, I found a solution in notes.

After my experience with selling my mother's property, I thought I'd suggest the idea of a seller second to my tenant-buyer. She was able to obtain a first mortgage, and I agreed to hold a small second mortgage. Since she'd bought the property with a seller assist, she was able to amortize her closing cost over 30 years with a balloon of $18,000 at the end of the five-year term. Another feature that didn't apply in this case because the buyer went FHA, this seller second can often let a buyer avoid mortgage insurance when purchasing the home, saving a monthly payment for the life of the loan. Here were the terms of that deal:

Principal balance: $18,000

Interest rate: 8.5 percent interest only

Term: Sixty months

Maturity date: October 9, 2014

Monthly payment: $127.50

First payment due: November 30, 2009

By utilizing a second mortgage and seller assist in this case, the tenant-buyer was able to purchase the property with no money out of pocket for a down payment and closing costs. It's nice that this strategy works for both investor-buyers and tenant-buyers, letting folks obtain their first property much sooner than through traditional means. What's funny is that her first lien payment and her second mortgage payment paid to me was actually less than the rent! Plus, by offering terms like this, I was able to sell the property without needing a Realtor, thus saving me 6 percent of the sale price.

Advantages for Sellers Carrying a Second

In the examples above, it's easy to see that there are many advantages for sellers offering secondary financing, such as:

- By offering terms to buyers, you can sell the rental property more easily, especially to another investor (as we did in the first example).
- Through these terms, you can possibly eliminate multiple costs.

The private sale from creative financing often eliminates the need for a Realtor as well as his or her commission fees. Plus sellers can offer a seller assist to buyers out of the money they save in these fees, making the sale more appealing. This type of financing can also lower the costs of transfer tax and capital gain tax.

- The sellers can continue to cash-flow after no longer owning the property. Making money without dealing with tenants, maintenance, inspections, and contractors is a wonderful thing.
- In the event of a default, the sellers are familiar with the asset they had once owned.

Advantages for Buyers Purchasing with a Seller-Second

- They can often buy a rental property with little or no cash out of pocket. If they're investor-buyers, this is extremely beneficial, since it gives them an infinite rate of return with zero cash into the deal. This also lets the investors build their portfolios faster and more easily than if they had to seek any sort of traditional or private financing.
- For the investor-buyers, the home is rent-ready without needing any downtime for a major renovation. In other words, it's a turnkey deal.
- For both the investor-buyers and tenant-buyers, all inspections by townships, home inspectors, wood infestation, etc., have all just been completed at the time of transfer or closing.
- Because of the lowered sales price, the buyers can also save on mortgage fees, transfer tax, and some insurances (i.e., PMI, homeowners, and title insurance).
- By not leaving any equity in the property, the investor-buyers are maximizing their yield on their total investment capital.

Selling on a Wraparound Mortgage

When I think back to one of my initial goals that I had from the first day I became an investor right up until I got into the note business, it was to get to twenty rental properties all paid off by age sixty-five. I figured everything would be gravy at that point, with twenty cash-flow streams pouring into my bank account each month. Plus I'd have options. I could sell one house a year (probably the one with the least amount of depreciation left) and live off that. Or, maybe better yet, I later thought I could sell a house a year with owner financing and make a nice stream of monthly cash flow, with a nice 10 percent down payment from the buyer. And if the note had some "seasoning" (where it performed for one year or more), I'd have a pretty salable note in case I needed liquidity. All without having to be in the landlord and maintenance business.

With such lofty dreams, you're probably wondering where the idea for the wraparound mortgage came in? To be up-front, the idea of the wraparound mortgage strategy was one of my safety nets. A wraparound mortgage is essentially when the seller leaves his or her current mortgage in place and creates a new mortgage with the buyer. So it's a way to sell your house with owner financing before your house is actually paid off.

If I were to sell one of my rentals to a buyer with a wraparound mortgage, we would create a new note with new terms, which is subject to my initial mortgage and actually "wraps around" this remaining, existing mortgage. Maybe the easiest way to describe this strategy is through example. If I sell this rental property for $150,000, and they gave me a 20 percent down payment ($30,000), I'm holding a mortgage for them of $120,000, even though I still owe $70,000 to my initial lender, regardless of transferring the deed at closing or upon final payment (i.e., like a wraparound land contract). So they pay me, and I pay the senior until it's eventually paid off.

Personally, I would prefer selling to a fellow investor's LLC because of compliance, since I would be creating a commercial note and mortgage instead of a more regulated owner-occupied residential loan. If I were to do an installment sale of the wraparound mortgage, depending on the location of the property, I'd most likely be able to defer my long-term capital gains, too, since the deed is escrowed and the title isn't transferred until the last payment is made. The beauty of the wraparound mortgage is that I don't have to wait until my traditional mortgages are all paid off to sell.

Leasebacks: An Alternative to Owner Financing

I feel as though a section on owner financing wouldn't be complete without at least mentioning the strategy of leasebacks. Leasebacks often serve as an alternative to owner financing. A leaseback is when an owner sells his or her property but decides to continue with the property as a tenant. This is another technique that I eventually learned is fairly common in commercial real estate. It's usually applied when a business owner owns his or her building and runs the business out of the location but has now decided to sell the property but will keep the business there.

A neighbor next to one of my multiunits had implemented this strategy in the past, and I found it to be quite interesting. The property itself was an old meatpacking plant when he purchased it. He had since converted it to quality office space with some commercial garages (some of which were built new, while others were retrofitted) and chose to run his plumbing and heating business out of one of the new garages. It wasn't too long before the crash of '08, and he saw the real estate market jump up in value, and since he was getting closer to retirement, he decided to sell at a high point. Even though he wanted to sell the property, he wasn't ready to stop his plumbing and heating business just yet. So he implemented a long-term lease for his business, and this leaseback situation was a win-win deal for the buyer, the seller, and him as a tenant. The new buyer bought a building with a built-in, dependable tenant, and the seller got a quality sales price while still being able to continue to run his business in the same location.

I've yet to personally have the opportunity to use a leaseback, but hey, it's a tool that's there for me in case I do. You may notice that, like leasebacks, many of these tools and note strategies I've outlined above come from commercial real estate investing, but in the grand scheme of this story, I haven't gotten there yet. Well, my next logical step was just that: commercial real estate.

CHAPTER 8
TAKEAWAYS

Always make multiple offers! My friend at the brokerage had the insight that you don't really know what motivates a motivated seller unless you make multiple offers, each of which has a unique appeal. Offering owner financing can be one of them.

My mom used a seller-second to sell her house...and cash-flowed for five years after selling it without any maintenance, tenants, township inspections, or headaches.

Wraparound notes demystified. Wraparound loans are notoriously hard to understand, but you can think of them as a new loan wrapped around an old loan, with a single payment covering both.

And don't forget leasebacks. Leasebacks can be a good strategy for you when selling a commercial property that you want to remain in as a tenant.

CHAPTER 9

Using Notes for Commercial Real Estate

OK, now we're at another major shift in my career. Until this point, I was in what I call accumulation mode with SFR properties, experiencing all the financing hurdles that came along with it. I was buying as much as I could get my hands on with as many conventional loans as I could get. Then, when those started to dry up, I was forced to get creative with financing soon after, and that wasn't always easy. After a while, though, I had reached one of my goals of attaining financial freedom. Now, it wasn't with one hundred or even twenty houses all paid off, but they were getting there (even with their HELOCs). Slowly but surely, my tenants were paying them off. And in the meantime, I could technically live off my rental income.

But my idea of financial freedom wasn't to just sit around. I was looking for something more, the next big thing. I continued to run into a few issues, however. For one, like many SFR investors, I was getting a lot of headaches with tenants, maintenance, and the townships (many of which were not landlord friendly, to put it lightly). Even with my property manager in place, it was still cumbersome. I was also trying to convince myself that I should be managing a handful of "easy" properties. After a while I was forced to ask myself, *Why am I standing in line at Home Depot*? Sure, being handy, I enjoyed some of the tactile work that came along with managing these properties, but what was this job really worth—$15/hour or $20/hour? Eventually my time didn't seem worth it compared with what I could be doing. And being in charge of an influential networking group, I started thinking bigger.

My First Commercial Building

I first ventured into commercial real estate before I even joined DIG. I did so with a small six-unit building in my local area of expertise. The owner of the property, a friend and my broker at the time, was motivated to sell after one of the tenants was involved with an attempted murder at the property. Yikes! That was the last straw for him! And for some crazy reason, it didn't deter me. In fact, I saw it as an opportunity to acquire a property from a motivated seller.

The property cash-flowed OK, but I didn't understand all the hype with commercial. However, after owning it for almost four years, I was starting to get into some hot water. I realized there were commercial necessities that were eating into my bottom line. After some careful consideration, I decided to remodel the building from six units to four, thus turning a commercial property into a residential one. What's funny is, I managed to collect the exact same amount of rent after this retrofitting. And the beauty of it all was that now my financing was much more favorable (with a lower rate and a longer term), my insurance dropped more than half in price, and I no longer needed a commercial municipal Dumpster (which was, back then, a costly $1,000/year expense). With the new conversion, I was also able to separate the utilities for every unit (another former costly expense), and since it was fewer units overall, my management fees were now less.

A few years later, I learned that with my commercial mortgage, the bank could have recast the loan around year five. I was fortunate to make these changes when I did because if I held it any longer, it would have been right around the time of the 2008 economic crash. With my main source of earned income being from my work as a Realtor, I really would have been in trouble. I say this because I eventually went from selling seventy-five houses a year as an investor-friendly Realtor to about seven. So if they were to recast my loan with my new (lower) income, I wouldn't qualify for my previous commercial financing, and they could call the loan in full or restructure it with less favorable terms. This could even lead to a foreclosure in the worst-case scenario. And since commercial residences under seventy to one hundred units require personal signing, I would be taking on that debt personally, which is lienable in a default and can become a personal liability. So I avoided all of that with this conversion.

All in all, I learned that smaller isn't always better in the commercial world, but my desire to move into that space was still there. I wanted to work in the world of larger-unit property, like apartment complexes, and I was well on my way to learning more about them when something happened. I was introduced to mobile home parks.

Mobile Home Parks

I've made it no secret that networking was beyond pivotal for my investing, so it will probably come as no surprise to learn that my path toward commercial real estate came from just that. Back in the early days of DIG and other smaller networking groups, it wasn't commonplace for investors to discuss their deals during the meeting, at least out loud. Since the meetings were in more of a classroom setting established by a nonprofit and full of newbies, it made sense that they were focused more on education. But there was hardly time for serious networking, and you didn't break bread with one another either. I always felt that last part was a shame, since it's such a simple way to really connect with someone. So along with a few colleagues of mine, I helped start our group, RING, as a direct response to that.

As RING grew, a few fellows came by to one of our subgroups and pitched me an idea—their mobile home park idea. It had never dawned on me to work in the mobile home space. But once they explained the investment, I found that in many ways, mobile home parks were appealing for multiple reasons. To name a few:

- There's less turnover because it's financially difficult for a mobile home owner to move out of a park. To give you an idea, it's usually anywhere from $3,000 to $5,000 to have a tractor trailer transport the property itself.
- There's less maintenance than for a building because you own just the land as opposed to the unit.
- There are no township fees (the mobile home owner pays things like use and occupancy fees, rental license fees, etc.), and the depreciation is more accelerated than with an apartment complex.

The trio who presented me the deal were all based in Stratford, New Jersey, and belonged to the same church. Through this religious bond came the desire to build a private Christian academy for grade school students. Being real estate investors, they devised a plan to build the school using the proceeds from various mobile home parks and storage facilities. They had a purpose bigger than themselves, which, *pro tip*, will almost always make it easier to raise private money, especially if it's for a charitable cause.

At the time they presented me the deal, they had already completed one storage center and one mobile home park project. They were looking to do more, but they needed someone to help with the fund-raising. They had done the previous deals with none of their own money and were continuing to do so for the next few parks. To do that, they needed to get creative, and since I had a very large network, they thought I'd be a natural fit. In exchange, I would not only learn how to properly raise serious capital on their dime, but I'd also gain a piece of the mobile home park investments. Together we did eight parks and two storage centers in total, raising both equity and debt for each.

Debt vs. Equity Financing for Commercial Real Estate Deals

Equity financing—*issuing additional shares of common stock to an investor.*

Debt financing—*borrowing money and not giving up ownership.*

When first venturing into commercial real estate—whether it's a deal with greater than four residential units, a mixed-use property, an office, or even an industrial space—investors may attempt self-funding initially, but what they soon realize is that if you plan to grow in commercial investing, you'll need money partners. When I was first approached with the mobile home park idea, I knew (and they knew) I didn't have much personal capital to invest—or at least enough to fully fund one or all of their planned projects—so I had to raise it elsewhere.

Although, I should deviate from this part in the story to add that I did personally invest later on, which proved to be a tool for me in raising private money. Showing investors you have skin in the game is never a bad idea and proves you believe in your investment, but I didn't know that quite yet. I was still learning how commercial financing really worked.

In Chapter 5, I wrote about how, when starting out, people tend to look for partners to do a real estate deal with. This is usually because they want to share risk within the deal, because they need more capital, or a combination of both. Since they're new, they don't always mind giving up equity in a deal. This can be a pretty big mistake, especially if you're the person who found the deal or you're the person doing the majority of the work. Usually capital is worth only paying a return of interest and points, not necessarily upside, especially in small residential deals. On the deal I described in my previous few chapters, I showed that through debt financing (with my cousin lending me money at 13 percent), it made much more sense to pay points on the money than to give up the equity, especially considering I still profit from the note on that property today.

How Most Commercial Deals Work Using Debt and Equity

There are plenty of instances in real estate where debt financing makes sense, but with larger deals that require more capital, as in the commercial world, it can become necessary to give up a portion of equity. Now, that doesn't mean debt is entirely out of the picture. Debt is usually used in the form of the primary loan obtained from a traditional bank or seller (e.g., owner financing), and the additional money required for the down payment, closing costs, and renovations or improvements is often raised in the form of equity. With larger down payments and lower loan-to-values, banks usually feel more comfortable to allow such creative financing. This mitigates their risk, not to mention that debt financing has a shorter term and higher interest rate than residential financing. With larger and larger deals, you'll usually see some variation of this play out, where it appears that the deal will share equity in the beginning but later changes to just debt in the future.

There are multiple profit centers in commercial real estate investing, but when putting together a deal, here's a common model you'll see:

No. 1. Find a viable commercial project. Whether you're dealing with apartments, mobile homes, offices, developments, or new construction, the numbers on the commercial deal need to make sense to be successful. Finding commercial deals can be just as easy or difficult as it is to find residential. Fortunately for us, we had a team enlisted to find parks; I was just in charge of the capital.

No. 2. Raise private equity. This is for the down payment (usually 20–30 percent), closing costs, and improvement/renovation costs. This is where I came in. We presented at real estate Q&As, hosted investor happy hours, toured the parks themselves, told friends and family, etc.

No. 3. Put an expert team together. This model includes advisers, an investment board, top management, middle management, on-site management, and a maintenance crew. Again, I was fortunate to basically plug into a team that was already in place. They assembled the team from the top down, starting with a commercial real estate broker who had decades of experience and specialized in mobile home parks, as well as a few other key members who brought in their expertise and recommendations.

No. 4. Obtain a 70–80 percent commercial loan. My partners had good credit, and the parks had solid numbers, so this was pretty simple for us. Some investors may need to utilize a money signer/cosigner if necessary, usually in exchange for equity. Keep in mind, these loans have higher interest rates than do residential loans, often amortize over twenty to twenty-five years (rarely thirty years), and will often recast in five to seven (or maybe even ten) years. Recasting isn't guaranteed, but it is a possibility because the property's value normally increases from the time of purchase while the loan balance decreases, and the investor team has usually improved the property.

No. 5. Purchase, improve, and then refinance. I'll get into how we did this below in our case study, but improvements are done to increase value, improve cash flow, and get better terms when refinancing. These improvements can include but obviously aren't limited to property renovation, updated landscaping/maintenance, a reduction in current vacancy rates, and rent increases (adjusted for the improvement of the overall property). These improvements tend to be done in approximately a three- to five-year period to enable a refinance and avoid possible recasting. The refinance is usually done for more favorable bank financing (and to take out any equity partners, thus retaining full ownership) unless the team is able to sell at a substantial profit along the way.

No. 6. Repeat. I didn't always know this was the common formula for how these deals went. I really wish someone had broken it down for me years earlier because once I learned it, it definitely demystified the process and got me unstuck. We used a very similar model for our mobile home park deals, except eventually we added notes to the mix.

CASE STUDY
A MOBILE HOME PARK IN WESTERN MICHIGAN

The company I worked for eventually owned and acquired a total of eight mobile home parks and two storage centers in multiple states. Nearly all the parks were more than one hundred units. I could probably write a whole book on all eight, but for simplicity's sake, let me walk you through one deal from start to finish—ending with how we used notes to generate more profits and wealth. This mobile home deal consisted of four separate parks and one storage center in western Michigan that my entity was a partner in.

Details on the Park
- 664 units, with 132 vacancies, on four manufactured housing communities near Lake Michigan
- One storage center, with additional RV and boat parking
- Current operational cash flow (from lot rent alone): $591,252
- Purchase price: $20.5 million
- Existing mortgage: $10.925 million, cross-collateralized assumable encompassing all four parks
- $4.5 million in capital required to close
- Significant tax write-off via fifteen-year depreciation schedules for park improvements (as opposed to thirty-nine years with building structures)
- The goal: increase cash flow to $1.189 million annually by year three, refinance by year five to return investment capital to investors, and sell by year fifteen, creating forced appreciation
- Minimum investment: $250,000 per investor (investors

own a combined loan-to-value of 80 percent; managing entity owns 20 percent)

Initial Financing for the Deal

The managing partners agreed to buy the property for the appraised value of $20.5 million. The original lender on the park was G.E. Capital, a bank and commercial lender based out of Chicago. Our team came in and assumed this existing commercial loan from the previous owner. This in and of itself was a current *traditional bank note* for $10.925 million—that first mortgage was the assumable part of the debt aspect of our deal. Taking over this was much more affordable and advantageous for our team than originating an entirely new loan from scratch. Because the property appraised for more money than the sale price, our company was able to take out a second mortgage for $5.475 million.

The rest was up to us, specifically my other money-raising partners and me. We were in charge of raising $4.5 million dollars in private money to close the deal. Investors were investing in shares of an LLC, with a minimum investment of $250,000. We held private dinners, did presentations, and took potential investors on park tours with follow-up visits throughout the renovation process and upon completion. Within a couple of months, we had enough accredited investors in our private placement to fund—this was the *equity financing* aspect of the deal. The investors were to be paid out of excess cash flow until the owners refinanced (approximately by year five), giving investors a tax-free distribution. The long-term (ten-to-fifteen-year) plan for our investors was to exit via sale or 1031 exchange because of depreciation tax advantages being diminished, unless the managing partners were to refinance again. With mobile home parks, since the majority of the investment is land leasing (and you cannot depreciate land), most of what you're depreciating is infrastructure (e.g., sewer/septic, roads, other improvements). This type of depreciation is more accelerated than with an actual apartment complex, where the commercial building itself is depreciated over thirty-nine years.

How We Would Raise the Value of the Park

The strategic plan was to increase the current positive cash flow of the park, thus increasing our monthly returns and the overall value. With 664 units total, there were still 132 lots vacant (equaling about 81 percent occupancy, or 532 units), with an average lot rent of $325/month. The short-term (three-year) plan was to increase rents on the mobile home units to an average of $375/month and to decrease vacancy to less than 10 percent, thus creating $643,200/year in additional cash flow after debt service. Sounds simple, right?

Two of the parks were also verified for expansion potential (sixty additional lots), which in turn could create approximately an extra $260,000/year in lot rent. That alone could significantly increase the community's value. There was great potential for future home sales too. The addition of pet and late fees would also generate an estimated $92,000/year.

These weren't the only other potential improvements that were uncovered during the due diligence process. Going back to the Robert Allen school of thought, there's almost always a way to refine and improve cash flow streams (and costly liabilities). For example, we believed we could do better on park insurance rates because we had a larger portfolio of commercial real estate than did the previous owner, enabling a new insurance provider to give us better rates because of an economy of scale. We also believed we could control legal expenses for things like zoning approvals and collections of bad debts, as well, since again, we had multiple parks. We used marketing strategies (e.g., free mobile home setup, free cable for six months, etc.) to attract residents, and we also believed that hosting community days and holiday celebrations would build a better sense of community and a better community of tenants/residents, which of course would result in more consistent lot rent.

How This Improved Value Can Help Refinancing

The mid-term (five-year) plan was to conduct a cash-out refinance of the existing mortgage after creating some forced appreciation with the above improvements that would increase the net operating income. Combining these improvements and increased lot rent with a plan to stabilize the expenses and decrease the number of vacancies would enable at least a 60–100 percent return of initial capital to investors. With much of their risk off the table, meanwhile, the investors continued to retain their same percentage of ownership going forward.

So in year five, if the mobile home parks' net operating income rose to about $1.189 million, we were looking at an appraisal of about $30 million. With that appraisal, we could potentially obtain a new refinance loan for approximately $21 million to $24 million, depending on what the bank would lend. We could then utilize this new loan to take out the original remaining balance of G.E. Capital's first and second mortgages (the remaining loan balance of which would have decreased by that time). Then we could use a portion of the remaining $6 million to $8 million to pay back the investors, while leaving the rest for reserves and expansion costs.

Utilizing Notes for Buying Additional Mobile Homes
So now we would own the park with the investors without the initial debt financing. We'd have the refinance loan to pay back, but that's done with increased cash flow now from a more valuable park. But there was still room for improvement, especially in terms of expansion.

It wasn't long before the New Jersey–based company that I was raising capital for acquired more than $30 million worth of commercial real estate, consisting of eight manufactured housing communities, one storage center, and several residential properties. They were also managing 1,300-plus units with properties that were located in Michigan, Indiana, and Pennsylvania. For this expansion, the plan was to purchase mobile homes to sell on vacant lots to incoming residents. Because the mobile home manufacturers didn't finance these homes themselves, we had to get creative. So we turned to notes yet again, this time by tapping into the equity of one of the parks and creating a preferred debt investment with a revolving business line of credit for a proposed amount of $600,000. This line of credit was a second mortgage note against the park funded by additional private investors. So this was a form of debt financing, funded by private investor capital, backed by equity. The investor terms were:

- Twelve-month/term per share
- $5,000/per share
- 15 percent interest-only payments, paid quarterly, with a principal balloon payment paid upon maturity
- With this capital, we purchased a variety of properties, new and used, all for varying prices. Some would sell for as low as $22,500 and others (depending on the quality) for up to $60,000. The benefit for investors' funding this line of credit was that they got a respectable preferred return that was passive, their investment was secured by property through a mortgage and promissory note, and in the event of a default, debt would get paid ahead of equity.

Profits from Selling Mobile Home Units with Notes

Since the mobile home manufacturers did not offer traditional financing, we found that through our business line of credit, we could do it ourselves, thus creating another profit center in the process. So with all incoming residents looking to purchase a home, our company utilized either owner financing or a similar rent-to-own system. The principals of my company always preferred committed residents rather than tenants because that usually meant a better, steadier cash flow.

Over a five-year period, we could potentially sell 232 homes (roughly twenty to twenty-eight sales/year). With our company's previous history, data showed that at least a quarter of incoming residents would purchase homes outright with cash (at a $15,000 profit with each sale). So fifty-eight homes at $15,000/home would be an $870,000 profit. Of the remaining 174 homes, we would sell each property with owner financing, utilizing contract notes with a 10 percent down payment. So just in down payments alone, that would give us an additional $783,000 in profit.

The estimated average cost for our company to purchase each home would be about $35,000 for a single-wide mobile home and $50,000 for a double-wide. The estimated sales revenue would vary with each home sale, but typically a homeowner would make a payment between $300 and $500 for a single-wide and $500 and $700 for a double-wide. The term for these payments was usually twelve years, though they could be as low as seven years depending on how significant the borrower's down payment was. At the end of the twelve-year term, a single-wide would typically yield our company anywhere from $50,400 to $72,000 if the home buyer were to complete his or her rent-to-own agreement. A double-wide would typically yield a $72,000 to $100,800 return.

Residents would make two payments to our company every month—one to go toward this owner-financing note and another to go toward monthly lot rent. The lot rent price would vary depending on the park and the land lease. This lot rent served as cash flow and, of course, raised the value of the park. Our company would also charge a management fee to each resident for on-site management, so naturally with more units in each park come more management fees. All these things quickly add up to some serious cash flow.

And remember, once these notes were sold, the revolving line of credit's balance would diminish and eventually get to zero, so we could do it all over again. The notes here served as a tool. They were a way to create additional profit centers to an already lucrative deal. We really utilized notes to help them acquire more homes faster and, in turn, homeowners who would pay more lot rent, fees, etc. All the while raising the overall value of the park, with the ultimate goal of selling with a significant value increase. But unfortunately, we never made it that far.

Where It Ended Up

The deal fell apart. All that work and all the proposed profits never came to fruition. The parks have since been foreclosed on. Sometimes that's life. Not every deal can be a
home run. But I learned pretty quickly that it's important
to understand why and learn from it.

What went wrong? To put it simply: Egos got in the way.
The upper management who organized the whole endeav-
or ended up suing each other. Two of the partners decided they didn't want to use the third partner's services for
renovations as originally planned, the third partner felt
snubbed, and eventually all three of them made a mountain out of a molehill. They could never settle it privately,
so it went to court.

I was lucky to have come out relatively unscathed financially compared with others, but I still lost about $250,000
after all was said and done. Though it certainly cost me
more than just money. I dedicated a large amount of my
time to the deal, years in fact, and it damaged my reputation in the process. Friends and colleagues lost money with
these parks, but I was fortunate that the majority of them
remain friends and colleagues of mine to this day. I think
part of that had to do with how the deal ended. I did my
absolute best to try to get their money back, hiring attor-
neys, filing lawsuits, and holding investor option meetings.
Above all else, I tried to stay in constant contact with my
investors to keep them in the know. I think the first instinct
of many fund-raisers may be to run and hide, but I found
being up-front and transparent was much appreciated. In
fact, many (though not all) of the same investors I brought
in on this deal stayed with me for future projects. I think
that communication and transparency had something to
do with it.

I also learned that going forward, I would need more
control. I couldn't continue to risk my reputation by the
whims of others, even if it was unintentional. The good
news was that after all of this, I was ready to do it again—
this time better than ever. The knowledge I'd absorbed

through this ordeal was priceless. I don't know if I could have spent $250,000 on formal education and gained the same amount of expertise. So now I had the connections, the fund-raising reputation, and the knowledge, and I was ready to do it all over again. Another project came quickly. I moved on to raising money for a large health and wellness center facility with attached commercial office condos in eastern Pennsylvania. They had very promising returns and an ace team in place, but then something happened that was out of everyone's control. The market crashed.

CHAPTER 9
TAKEAWAYS

Bigger isn't always better in commercial real estate. I found with my six-unit that it was less risk and more advantageous to my bottom line to convert my commercial property into a residential one.

Mobile home parks. My first serious capital-raising experience came for a project I wasn't looking for but that found me. The benefits of mobile home park investing include less turnover, less maintenance (since you don't own a building), and no township fees!

Debt versus equity financing for commercial deals. The two main ways to raise capital are via debt and equity, and for many commercial projects, they're often used together.

The classic six-step recipe for success in commercial investing. Find a project, raise private equity, put an expert team together, obtain a commercial loan for 70–80 percent of the financing, purchase/improve/refinance, repeat.

Case study: Michigan mobile home park. This case study breaks down exactly what the numbers were and shows how we utilized notes to maximize this commercial deal.

How to survive a deal gone south. Despite the soundness of the business model, this venture crashed and burned because of conflicts between the principals. The main lesson learned was to take care of your investors and stay in communication every step of the way.

CHAPTER 10
Institutional Notes

Finally! Right? I know it took ten chapters for you to get here, but hey, it took me about twenty years of investing! Good things come to those who wait, and we're both fortunate to discover one of the greatest investments in the world. Until this point in the book, I've focused mainly on how notes can help finance and amplify all different types of real estate investments, from commercial to residential, but what I've yet to do is highlight the institutional note business in and of itself. And that's because, well, it's a whole entire industry in and of itself! Though it wasn't as foreign as I'd once thought. It did involve financing and banking, but it was still an investment backed by hard real estate, and that I definitely understood. So how did a guy like me, a former contractor/Realtor/investor, end up in the world of hedge funds and banks? Easy. Through real estate, of course. Unfortunately, it had to come during one of the biggest economic crises the world had seen since the Great Depression.

Calm Before the Storm

The Wellness Center project we were working on contained a variety of spaces related to the health and wellness industry. Everything from a retail pharmacy to a fitness center. It also contained a large amount of potential commercial office condos. The location and demographic were pitch-perfect to fill this type of space with the appropriate clientele. But with the financial downturn, businesses quickly halted expansion. So after securing the land, gaining approvals of the townships, creating blueprints, and raising the private equity for the deal, I watched the market shift. The bank wanted at least 60 percent of the units leased or sold prior to providing the funding for the construction, which wasn't uncommon. But with the recession halting expansion and business growth, we couldn't find the proper buyers or occupants. The deal fell apart and stayed empty for almost the following ten years, until it was sold at a loss. So once again, a case of a good investment going bad.

Bob, one of the future cofounders of my note company PPR, was a fund-raising partner in this project with me. In fact, he was also raising private money for the mobile home parks, which is actually where I met him. Just like me, Bob had come from a real estate background, though he also specialized in franchise businesses. He was the first person I met when I flew into western Michigan to see the potential parks and storage facilities we were thinking of investing in. He picked me up from the airport to show me around, and though we didn't know each other at the time, we learned a few minutes into our conversation that we happened to live only about twenty minutes from each other back in Pennsylvania! It's funny how small the world can be sometimes. After the deal went south, we remained friends, and he came on to the Wellness Center project. He also attended some of my RING meetings. John, my other future cofounder at PPR, was also a part of RING. He was an investor, too, but had more of a corporate real estate background and worked in lending. John was introduced to me and our group through a mutual friend, and he eventually became my mortgage lender.

A few years before we formed our business, all three of us were at a meeting I hosted with a fund manager from New York City. Based on Wall Street, he spoke to our group about a little-known concept called...institutional note investing. He outlined the investment, as was custom for all our speakers to do, and explained how the mortgage business was a trillion-dollar industry.[11] But until that time, investing in these assets wasn't common for the everyday investor. He was looking to bridge that gap by purchasing and investing in delinquent assets, specifically delinquent junior lien assets. Junior

---

11 Louise Story, "Home Equity Frenzy Was a Bank Ad Come True," *New York Times*, published August 14, 2008, http://www.nytimes.com/2008/08/15/business/15sell. html?_r=1&hp=&oref=slogin&pagewanted=all&mtrref=www.felixsalmon.com.

liens (or second mortgages, as they're commonly referred to) weren't as common as you might think back then, and I still meet people who aren't familiar with them. Junior liens can be a multitude of things, including any mortgages subordinate to the senior lien, lines of credit, or home equity loans.

The reason for such variety in the nomenclature of these liens is that each one has morphed and changed over time. The phrase "home equity loan" has been around since at least the time of the Great Depression, but the transformation of the idea of "second mortgage" began in earnest in the 1970s and early 1980s. Banks were looking to create additional income, and when marketing executives at banks and lending institutions realized that "second mortgage" had an unappealing ring to it, they seized the idea of "home equity," with its connotations of ownership and fairness. Since then, the value of home equity loans outstanding has ballooned from more than $1 billion to more than $1 trillion, with nearly a quarter of Americans who have first mortgages also having some variation of a junior lien today.[12]

The fund manager's strategy was basically to gather private capital from investors (like ones in our group) to purchase pools, or "tranches," of these second mortgages from banks looking to get them off their books. These were different from the owner-financed (or seller-financed) notes I had seen in the past. These were notes originated or underwritten by a bank, so it was "cleaner" paper that could come from direct institutions (i.e., banks), and so there was a much larger supply. Basically these notes were delinquent because the borrowers had ceased payment. The fund manager's company would have a loss mitigation team in place to try to rehabilitate the asset and get the performance of said asset back on track. So after purchasing, he would work through some of these assets (to try to make delinquent notes re-perform), then sell some if not all of the assets, paying back the investors with a portion of the returns and keeping whatever was left. At its core, it was actually a revolutionary and simple idea. And what do I do when I hear a new, revolutionary idea? That's right—nothing! But this time, I was lucky because my one future partner, John, did.

---

12 Story, "Home Equity Frenzy."

The Perfect Storm

Just before the real estate market nearly came to a halt with the 2008 recession, I was again looking for a change. My two major commercial endeavors that Bob and I were raising money for weren't taking off as planned, and we all sensed something was changing in the market. Being a lender, John could see the writing on the wall with how loans were being underwritten and the lack of loans he personally was underwriting. I could see it, as well, being an investor and working with borrowers as an investor-friendly Realtor. My investing friends and I were already purchasing fewer and fewer properties because of declining values and our main exit strategy of refinancing being removed from the table because of more-severe lending restrictions.

I was selling a fraction of the properties I had in previous years. And without sales to funnel, my title company was eventually forced to close. Without investors buying properties, my property management income stream started to dissipate as well. My brokerage even folded and was absorbed by another firm that didn't allow for property management. Even for a private lender, it was getting worse, since the lack of a refinance option led to a higher default rate among borrowers. Private lending was already a tough option for deploying capital anyway, since the legal requirements limit the amount of private notes that can be originated per year for an individual. Lending to entities or LLCs, which I often did, also became much more restrictive because of usury laws and origination requirements involving extensive underwriting and due diligence. Not to mention, the duration of most private notes is fairly short (twenty-four months or less), leaving investors like me constantly searching for the next borrower and another deal to deploy capital. So scaling this type of business in that market especially was proving to be difficult.

My old model of multiple streams of income was slowly starting to fall apart. I couldn't even go back to painting because of my injury. And even if I could, new construction had screeched to a halt! I was fortunate to have my properties keep me afloat, but without the ability to obtain traditional bank financing or even a hard money loan to buy more properties, I needed something new. So with nowhere to turn, I had to adapt. Fortunately, this was the exact same time John had asked Bob and me to lunch to discuss a new business opportunity.

PPR Is Born

We knew the crash was coming, only we didn't know the full extent of it. What we did know was there would be a lot of delinquent mortgages about to hit the market. John had invested some money in this note fund a few years prior and was earning consistently healthy returns. More important, he'd started to understand the business model behind delinquent notes and saw an opportunity to create something similar. The only problem was, John didn't have the start-up capital, and the only people he knew who could raise money were, you guessed it, his friends from RING. Unknown to us, John had a plan when he set up a meeting between Bob and me to pitch his new idea. His idea: to form our own note company. Bob and I would raise the money, and John would analyze and handle the assets (obviously our roles at PPR have since changed). After he explained to us what he knew about the business, we agreed to form an entity and purchase our first few notes.

We bought just four delinquent second mortgage notes to start. To make a long story short, one note was a grand slam in terms of profitability, one was a home run, and two we lost money on. How we did this taught us a few lessons. The first is (and we learned this the more we worked in the note business) that note buying is statistical. Not every deal is going to be a success, and with junior liens especially, you never truly know your exit strategy until you talk to the borrower. If we had bought only the two disaster loans, I might not be writing this book right now. We also started to learn from our mistakes with the two assets that had gone south. But overall we saw enough potential in this model that we decided to raise money to buy more notes. Once I started to see the passive income from these, without all the headaches of my past ventures, I decided to change my goal of one hundred houses to one hundred notes—but I would soon learn that this goal was much too small for where we'd end up.

CHAPTER 10
TAKEAWAYS

The crash (a.k.a. the perfect storm). The Great Recession was the biggest shake-up the real estate market had seen in decades, and thankfully, despite its challenges, it changed my personal course as an investor toward the world of notes.

What are junior liens? Second mortgages, HELOCs, lines of credit, any mortgage subordinate to the senior lien.

PPR is born! PPR came into being by accident, and we started out as a small-scale investing "experiment."

CHAPTER 11
How Institutional Notes Work

From my time at DIG, and through my work with both private lending and seller-financed notes, I understood what a note was and how it worked in essence. It wasn't until we started working in the business that we came to fully understand the full cycle of an institutional note before it came to us, the note buyers. Understanding the process is key to note buyers because knowing where a note has been, how it originated, and how it could end up nonperforming will help determine future strategy. And understanding how the bank deals with these notes will help with due diligence and buying, among other things.

Earlier I defined what an institutional mortgage and a note are as a recorded document (the mortgage itself) that attaches the loan (the note, also known as a lien) against real property, securing it. This note serves as a contract in which the borrower agrees to repay a certain portion of the loan to the payee or lender within a set period of time and under specific terms (e.g., interest rate, penalties, etc.). Almost like a tree, there exist many branches of notes that vary in type and lien position, but no matter the category of asset, all institutional mortgage notes start with a borrower. This is where these notes go from here.

Lifecycle of a Loan

Before a note ever reaches a note buyer's hands, an investor should know a note's origins and the lifecycle of a loan.

As I mentioned, a borrower is behind all notes. More than half of all Americans walk into a bank's or mortgage broker's office in hopes of obtaining a home mortgage, a home equity loan, or a line of credit. From there, a loan can follow only two major paths—it can remain a performing note or become a nonperforming note (NPN).

THE LIFE OF A NOTE

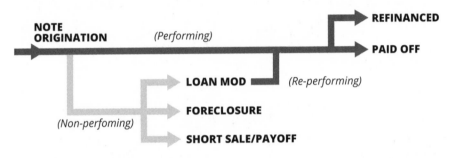

The note may be sold at any point or phase.

Based on a graphic created by Ryan Krail of Lightmark Media

Two Paths for a Note

A residential loan follows only two major paths—it can remain a performing note or become a nonperforming note.

- **Performing note (also referred to as a re-performing note):** a loan on which payments of interest and principal are being made. In the eyes of the bank, notes are still considered performing if they are less than ninety days past due.
- **Nonperforming note:** a loan that is in default or close to being in default. Many loans become nonperforming after being in default for three months, but this can depend on the contractual terms.

If a Loan Performs

In a normal market, nearly all loans perform, and when they do, there are generally two directions a performing loan can take:

1. The borrowers keep the loan and diligently make payments until they sell or refinance their home.

OR

2. The borrowers keep the loan and diligently make payments until the mortgage reaches maturity.

Note: Our data tell us the "payoff at maturity" option is less likely because the average homeowner sells or refinances his or her home within five to seven years after purchase.

Occasionally banks and other institutions will sell these performing loans to large servicers, brokers, loan exchanges, or even an individual investor. But the majority of notes that go to market and make up the industry go through the next process—from nonperforming to re-performing status.

If a Loan Is Nonperforming

In a small percentage of loans, an unforeseen circumstance occurs in the life of a borrower that causes him or her to stop paying. What generally happens in this case is that the borrower pays down a loan for a certain number of years until an unexpected event disrupts his or her life, such as a death, a divorce, a job loss, a medical emergency, or any combination of these events. This causes the borrower to be unable to afford to make his or her payments, and the bank has to make a decision.

Impact of a Default on the Bank

At this point, the bank is stuck with a nonperforming asset that can affect its reserve requirements, thus impeding its lending abilities. Most banks will consider a loan to be delinquent, or nonperforming, after ninety days of nonpayment. This leaves the bank with several options for this nonperforming loan, which could include:

- The bank can modify the loan.
- The bank can accept a short sale.
- The bank can accept a discounted payoff from the borrower.
- The bank can obtain a deed-in-lieu, in which the borrower signs the property over to the bank.

- The bank can foreclose, with the bank typically liquidating the property (selling the home as an REO property).
- The bank can sell the note and mortgage to a third party.

Working with the Banks

The primary reason banks sell loans is for liquidity, and it's with this option that I, and other note investors, come into play. Although some banks may service their own delinquent loans, it's usually easier for many banks to liquidate their notes through a trade desk, a loan exchange, or a brokerage. Depending on the lending institution, there are many reasons to seek liquidity: tax payments, legal fees, loan loss reserve requirements because of a particular asset's performance, or even just loss mitigation overload. It's this discount that a note buyer obtains at purchase that creates the opportunity for the note buyer to have more flexibility when exiting the note.

How Notes Are Sold

The majority of banks facilitate the sale of notes through loan exchanges and trade desks. Exchanges and trade desks essentially serve as platforms to buy and/or sell notes to approve vetted buyers. Many trade desks are in-house for banks and specialty servicers, while some smaller community banks and individual note sellers utilize loan exchanges. Occasionally notes are sold on what is known as a loan-level basis (one at a time), but more often, they are sold in larger portfolio packages containing hundreds or even thousands of loans. Though this may sound like a lot, nonperforming loans generally make up only a small percentage of a bank's overall portfolio. This is where the cycle ends for the bank, but for the investor, this is actually where it all begins.

CHAPTER 11
TAKEAWAYS

There are two paths for a note: performing and non-performing.

Why borrowers may default. An unexpected event disrupts their life, such as a death, a divorce, a job loss, a medical emergency, or any combination of these events.

The primary reason banks sell notes. In a word: liquidity.

How banks sell notes. Through loan exchanges and trade desks.

CHAPTER 12

Advantages of Investing in Institutional Notes

When Bob, John, and I started in notes, we didn't know all the advantages they had to offer. We just knew that this endeavor could definitely be a viable business. We also knew that the three of us were almost the equivalent of unemployed and that to start this business, we didn't need much, which you'll see comes into play with some of the advantages below. In fact, we didn't even have an office when we started. We were all working out of our own houses and essentially working for speculative pay at best. But we had hope, we had two successful deals under our belt, and we felt as though we were learning the business. With the impending economic downturn, there was also a lot of talk about a large supply of delinquent junior liens coming down the pike. So we decided to take the plunge.

We started specifically in the junior lien space because these assets sold for a cheaper price point (which required less capital to get started), there was much less competition in the junior space as opposed to the senior lien space, and the supply was abundant (and growing). Many of these advantages were factors of the marketplace at that time; if we started today, these advantages and our strategy would probably be different. But universally speaking, they weren't the only reason we jumped in and have remained in the note space over the past decade. The major advantages for investing in both senior and junior liens remain largely the same. If I had to condense all of these into just a handful of things, here's what they would be:

Advantage No. 1—Passive Cash Flow

For me, owning hard real estate always had and still does offer many great tax advantages, especially when including depreciation deductions that can offset positive cash flow. Although I consider my real estate to be passive from an IRS tax perspective, what many people including me have failed to realize is how much *active* work is required in managing and maintaining property. For the owner/landlord, active work can include everything from dealing with tenants and their liability to maintenance and townships, as well as the ever-increasing property taxes. Even for those of us who own property "hands-free" through turnkey investments or outsourced property management, we still may find that managing the managers can be work.

Owning a Performing Note Is Easier than Owning a House

When a note is re-performing and being repaid by the original borrower, the holder of the note will receive payments every month with little or no work required, making his or her investment entirely passive.

- When notes are paid off early, also known as a cash-out, they can be great short- to medium-term investments, with the entirety of the balance owed paid to an investor before maturity. This can be anywhere from a few months to a few years.
- When paid until maturity, many notes offer a very significant profit over the course of many years, especially considering that most mortgages have terms with decades' worth of monthly payments.
- Whether the balance is paid back in monthly installments, a lump sum, or a combination of the two, re-performing notes offer a fairly predictable profit.

Advantage No. 2—Volume and Control

Although I bought residential property mostly locally, I did venture into commercial real estate in other parts of the country. Despite the successes and failures of the investments, managing people and properties in other areas proved to be both tiresome and inconvenient. Even owning and managing residential properties locally could prove cumbersome beyond a certain amount of properties.

Owning a Note Portfolio Is Easier than Owning a Property Portfolio

Managing a portfolio of notes is much easier than managing a large portfolio of properties for the following reasons:

- A note portfolio (either performing or nonperforming) can be managed from the phone and computer without ever requiring you to leave the house or office. This lets servicers manage notes on properties across the nation.
- Fortunately, you're less likely to have to deal with a lot of tenants and maintenance issues, since notes deal more with the paper behind the property.
- In the rare instance that there are these issues, we have what is known as mortgage servicers and property preservation companies in the note industry. Servicers handle not only accounting and payment management but also any issues that arise with the resident. Property preservation companies deal with any physical issues with the property.

Advantage No. 3—Notes Are Profitable in Various Market Conditions

Unlike the volatility of the stock market, note prices in the marketplace function in relation to supply and demand and are directly correlated with real estate values. So in an up market, when the economy is in full swing and there are fewer foreclosures and home prices are high and climbing:

- There is a smaller supply of delinquent notes available in banks' portfolios, allowing the banks to gain a higher price for their notes, especially because all notes are more likely to be fully covered by equity.
- Although investors might have a higher acquisition cost, they now benefit from a quicker exit. When there's a question of time versus money, the adage "A fast nickel beats a slow dime" is proved true. What's better, a 50 percent return in three months or a 150 percent return in twelve months?

Conversely, in a down market there are more delinquent assets available (along with more junk assets), and there is less equity in the marketplace.

In a down market...

- It takes longer to exit a deal because there are fewer buyers for an asset backed by a property that may be dropping in value or has little remaining value.
- Down markets create more assets in the marketplace for less capital invested. For the same amount of money in an up market, a note investor could acquire a larger quantity of assets in a down market.
- Even if there is little to no equity, as the market improves, so does the value of a note investor's portfolio.

Advantage No. 4—Collateral

Unlike owning stocks that offer no real collateral, real estate is one of the safest investments on the market, since the investment itself is actual physical property. It wasn't until I learned about notes that I discovered there was an investment option that offered a very similar style of security.

Since a performing note is secured by real, physical property, there are multiple means of protecting a note investment:

- Owning a secured lien that is tied to property, especially if the property has equity, involves little or moderate risk because a note owner has a right to foreclose on the property and to recoup some or all of the initial investment. The investor who owns the note has a claim on the property just as the bank would if it were to own the note.
- Unlike in an eviction, in a default of a property with equity, the note owner could recover missed payments, late fees, attorney fees, and corporate advances at a future date.
- Even junior liens with no equity or low equity can still be viable investments because the borrower usually has a vested interest in the property, and traditional equity may not always be the sole factor when it comes to remaining in the home.

Advantage No. 5—Versatility

My favorite aspect about investing in property or hard real estate has always been all the opportunities it affords me for making a profit. What many real estate investors may not know is that nearly all the forms of profitability property ownership offers may be found with notes.

What You Can Do with a Note

Not only can purchasing notes be a unique way to obtain property, especially when buying vacant first mortgages, but notes can also be flipped, rehabbed, and borrowed against or leveraged like real estate.

- **Flipping or wholesaling a note.** Whether a note is performing or nonperforming, it can potentially be sold in any condition to an investor at any time. Generally, a note is not required to be held for a certain amount of time before it can be sold again.

  In an up market, for example, someone could purchase a performing note and hold on to it for a few months as he or she collects payments, later selling it for close to, if not the same as, the purchase price. More important, the note doesn't need to be performing to be sold either.

- **Partial.** Another strategy to recapitalize is by selling what is known as a partial. This practice refers to selling a partial amount of payments to an investor for a designated term at a designated price. This option can be a great way to quickly recover a portion of the initial investment while still maintaining ownership of the note. It is beneficial for the partial note buyer, as well, because it requires a smaller amount of money to invest for a shorter period of time.

- **Rehabilitating a note.** Like a house, notes can be rehabbed or retouched by reworking the original note. If a borrower were to miss one or more payments because of an unforeseen circumstance, the note owner has the ability to rework the terms of the loan to fit the borrower's new needs. This allows the borrower to stay in the home while also maintaining a steady cash flow to the investor.

- **Borrowing against the note.** The most versatile strategy of note investing involves an investor's best friend, *leverage.* Since the note is generating monthly income for the investor, it can be considered a cash-flowing asset. As an asset, this note can then be used as collateral for a loan with a private money investor; this is known as a collateral assignment of note and mortgage.

  Just as a motor vehicle is collateral for an auto loan, a performing note can be collateral for a private investor loan. In fact, the private investor loan allows the investor to recapitalize in a tax-free manner. Since this is a loan, the new private money creates an opportunity for a revenue stream that is exponential because the loan can be used to purchase more notes.

Advantage No. 6—Socially Conscious Investing

One thing that always attracted me to real estate was the fact that everyone needs a home, and through my rentals or flips, in some way I was responsible for helping families find homes. With notes, investors are helping borrowers stay in their homes without incurring any more debt that could cause further repercussions down the road. Unlike stocks, which are a zero-sum game with investors playing either side of the investment, always leaving one party at a loss, notes can be advantageous for not only the investor but also every party involved.

How Note Investing Can Be Beneficial

- Borrowers benefit from working with note buyers to create a viable solution to stay in their property or move on and/or buy time without incurring debt that can be detrimental to their financial life.
- Banks benefit from others investing in notes, as well, because they are able to remove what is considered to be "toxic" assets off their books, therefore giving them greater power to do what they do best: lend money.
- Housing makes up a large percentage of the economy, and reforming distressed debt in that area is beneficial to the entire economic system. When people are not paying their mortgage, they're also not paying their taxes or insurance escrowed in their mortgage. By turning these delinquent mortgages into performing ones, note investors not only help individuals through their financial struggles but also help improve the community at large.

So with all these advantages, who wouldn't want to add note investing to his or her portfolio? Of course, these benefits don't necessarily mean note investing is always easy. Nonperforming notes still need to be rehabilitated into re-performing status, and an exit strategy still needs to be agreed on with the borrower before any sort of recapitalization begins. So what's the next step in that process? Well, you need to find a note first.

CHAPTER 12
TAKEAWAYS

Cash flow without ownership? Yes! Owning real estate has advantages, but notes give you a way to get similar cash flow without the headaches of managing properties and tenants.

Other advantages of notes compared with properties. Notes are great for their scalability, ease of management, profitability in various market conditions, and versatility.

Notes are more like real estate than you think. Whatever you can do to a property (flip, rehab, refinance/borrow against, sell, etc.), you can also do with a note.

The bigger picture: socially conscious investing. I make the case that note investing can be good for business and good for society.

CHAPTER 13
Where to Find Notes

When I tell people about my business now and they want to get involved, one of the first questions they ask me is "Where do I find notes?" I often wish I had someone to simply tell me that answer when we started out! I suppose the best way to answer that question is by saying it's a lot like real estate, meaning there could be opportunities anywhere, and there's more than just one way to buy.

That said, if you're searching for institutional nonperforming notes, it would seem that the natural place to find them for sale would be banking institutions. Starting out, my partners and I thought the same thing, but we quickly learned that although many banks do originate, buy, and sell nonperforming notes, for a single note buyer (especially a loan-level buyer), banks can be one of the most difficult places to purchase from. The majority of banking institutions implement buying requirements that vary depending on the bank. These could include proof of funds, references, a documented trade history, and even meeting current regulatory requirements. Not to mention you have to be able to get in touch with the bank's correct trade desk. Which isn't as simple as picking up the phone book and calling in. And when dealing with larger institutions, departments within the same company or relative branch may not even speak to one another, so it can a challenge, to say the least. These hurdles and requirements are understandable, though. The banks can't take the PR risk of selling to just any individual off the street. Because of this, it is often easier to purchase notes from a fund, broker, or servicer.

Note Buying Is All About Relationships

Fortunately, in the beginning, after working with the note seller who taught us the business, we were connected with other note brokers. Though there were many false starts and a lot of fragmentation within the marketplace itself, we didn't let that deter us. What we realized was one of the most important parts about finding notes: It's a relationship-based business. As we grew, we started expanding our network to other specialty servicers, serious brokers, and eventually large banks, financial institutions, and government agencies (or government-sponsored enterprises).

Today, we use all types of networking tactics, both online and in person, to consistently generate sources of notes. Networking events both locally and nationwide for real estate investing, distressed debt, and the banking industry can be important gateways into the note-seller community. Some websites such as LinkedIn and Bigger-Pockets (the publisher of this book) offer subgroups dedicated to note investing, while others such as Meetup integrate both online and local networking to connect those interested in working with notes all over the United States.

Sources for Notes

There's no need to sit around and wait for a meeting to start when you can connect with people at the touch of a button. Online, not only can new note buyers connect directly with others in the industry, but they can also join groups to ask questions and find notes for sale. Many note groups on the web have notes listed for sale on an individual or small-pool basis that are usually sold by either other note investors or brokers.

Note Brokers

In some cases, a note-buying transaction can occur directly between a note buyer and a note seller, but other times, someone else facilitates the connection. This person is known as a broker, and much like a bank, he or she charges points (percentage of the purchase price) for his or her services. It's important to note that brokers usually fall into one of two categories: The first kind of broker has access to product and is solely trying to benefit from positioning himself or herself in a deal and charging a markup fee. The second kind of broker, although still charging a fee, has an ongoing relationship with a large number of note buyers and banking institutions. This type of broker also facilitates the sale in a compliant way and may even assist the note buyer after the transaction is complete if any problems arise, like missing documents, collateral, etc. The second kind of broker is usually interested not only in the sale but also in future business and can be paid a fee by the buyer, the bank, or both. Although both types of brokers may gain access to assets available for purchase, it's usually the latter type that remains a long-term, reliable connection to note sources.

We found our first note broker through our initial note seller. When we went into business purchasing and managing notes, our broker friend went in a different direction, connecting note buyers with note sellers. Our network of brokers also grew from online connections, such as loan exchanges and social media, as well as through word-of-mouth recommendations from other note sellers and even fellow note buyers. It took many years and a good amount of private capital to circumvent brokers and get in touch directly with a bank. Buying from a bank isn't necessary for every type of note buyer. Individuals could potentially find plenty of product simply through brokers, along with the following three sources.

Loan Exchanges

Some smaller community banks and even some large banks without trade desks in-house often have notes to sell, but they don't always have the means to do so in an efficient way for the best possible price. In this situation, they employ what is known as a loan exchange. Loan exchanges don't always require a direct personal connection, and they have online venues for purchasing notes, making it much easier for note buyers to find institutional assets. Most loan exchanges are open to the public but do require registration and some form of vetting approval.

Servicers

Servicers operate in a similar manner to loan exchanges, by providing an online note sale platform or "trade desk" to the general public. The difference is that the assets are managed by the servicer rather than brokered through an exchange. Servicers can be a great place for new buyers to find and analyze product.

Note Funds

Unlike a servicer or a loan exchange, note funds usually take title to all their assets, possibly even creating re-performing loans out of nonperforming loans. Unless publicly traded, note funds usually pool money from private investors to participate in large mortgage purchases, using a leverage strategy that's similar to the bank's "net interest margin" concept. This bulk purchasing, in effect, gives the company access to wholesale pricing. This benefit may even be reflected in the purchase price of assets to note buyers. Note funds serve as an intermediary, moving wholesale product downstream, ending at the retail market.

Just like buying that first piece of real estate, taking the leap to find and buy that first note is usually the most difficult. It's important to remember that as time goes on and a note buyer continues in the business, his or her track record begins to grow, making note seller connections much easier to discover. But you don't want to purchase just any note that comes your way. Once an investor finds a note to purchase, he or she must know how to determine whether it's the right note for him or her to buy.

CHAPTER 13
TAKEAWAYS

Buying notes is all about relationships. Buying and selling notes isn't purely transactional. Both parties—buyer and seller—base their decisions partly on the other's reputation and track record.

Sources of notes to buy: note brokers, loan exchanges, servicers, note funds.

What about note funds? Note funds not only sell notes directly to investors but also provide a way to invest in a pool of notes by participating in the fund.

CHAPTER 14
Due Diligence for Note Buyers

Note buying isn't always smooth sailing. My business partners and I found that to be the case when we started in the business. Being in such a niche and fragmented market, we had dealt with more than one unscrupulous note seller over the years at PPR. So we've learned it's best to be prepared. Due diligence varies for both the type of note and the position it is in, making it a necessary step prior to purchasing any asset. The first place to start, no matter the type of asset, is with the note seller. It's vital to know and trust the note seller. Just as banks need to perform their due diligence when finding buyers, note investors need to do the same when choosing their note sellers. If an investor is purchasing from a seller he or she doesn't know, it's especially important to put safeguards in place before deciding to move forward with a trade.

Vet the Seller

Thoroughly vetting an unknown or new note seller can be done in multiple ways:
- Complete a **background check** on the seller (and his or her partners if possible) to look for any past criminal activity, prior judgments, etc.
- **Ask others in the note-buying community** about their previous transactions with the seller. This could help an investor understand the seller's purchase process, collateral delivery, etc.
- **Require a bailee letter.** This letter identifies an individual who

temporarily gains possession but not ownership of a property under a contract or bailment.

- **Ask for an exception report.** This is essentially a collateral inventory report, usually done by a third-party document custodian, used to reference any documents that may be missing.
- **Escrow some or all of the funds until the deal is complete.** Involving a third party who can facilitate the transaction, such as an escrow attorney or another type of custodian, lets note buyers review all the collateral prior to finalizing the purchase.

Note sellers aren't always 100 percent accurate with information on the assets they sell. And sometimes there are mistakes, so it's important to do research and verify their information. When analyzing what information the seller is providing, keep in mind that sometimes the status, equity, or value of notes can fluctuate. If the seller has provided data that prove incorrect, it could end up being unfavorable for the unknowing note buyer. For a note buyer who knows what to look for, it could also mean getting a great deal or creating a situation in which the investor could negotiate a lower price.

Performing Notes

With performing notes, whether they're first or second mortgages, experienced note investors tend to focus on four things:

- **Borrower's pay history.** A solid pay history is important because the longer a note pays, the more the odds of a default usually decrease, which affects a note's classification and pricing. The same rule of thumb applies for arrears payments, which can show how financially committed a borrower is to his or her new payment plan.
- **Credit.** Evaluated at origination, this can be used to study the trends of a borrower's credit in relation to his or her other current bills. With second mortgages, the most important factor a credit report provides is the senior lien status.
- **Equity.** Equity in the property securing the note backs up an investor's capital; if for some reason the borrower were to re-default, then the note owner would most likely have to foreclose, exiting through the property.

- **Geography.** When buying a first mortgage or a high-equity second lien, an investor may be more concerned with geography for a variety of reasons, including determining foreclosure costs and timelines that differ from state to state, as well as demographics, population, and job growth. The real estate market and local economy also vary by location.

Nonperforming Notes

No matter what type of lien is being purchased, it's absolutely necessary to know the value, the property, the borrower's intent, and the potential exits.

Due Diligence with NPN (Nonperforming Note) First Mortgages (Senior Liens)

Specifically for first mortgages, due diligence items can include:
- **Value (fair market value, or FMV):** Determining value is critical, since it shows how much equity is backing the property.
- **Title and occupancy:** An investor should obtain an occupancy and encumbrance report to determine liens, ownership, and occupancy status.
- **Taxes, insurance, municipal liens, and homeowner association or condo association (HOA) fees:** Depending on the note and its location, any of these can be risk factors because said fees could be lienable in some states.
- **Location, comparables, property condition:** Obtaining a broker price opinion is recommended to validate location and to try to get an idea of the neighborhood and/or property condition. It can help determine occupancy and value as well.

Due Diligence with NPN Second Mortgages (Junior Liens): Equity vs. No Equity

Due diligence on residential junior liens can vary dramatically depending on the type of lien. For example, high-equity second liens require due diligence similar to that of a first lien because they're more expensive and backed by equity. These junior liens go through a similar foreclosure process, leaving investors with a favorable outcome even if they have to exit through the property.

When you're looking to purchase a no-equity second mortgage, there are a few other factors to consider:

- **Senior lien status:** One of the most important indicators of borrower intent, senior lien status and monitoring is important for all second liens but especially for no-equity seconds. This is because when a borrower is current on his or her senior lien, it tells the investor two things: The borrower likely has a source of income and a desire to stay in the property. This is typically verified by pulling a credit report.
- **Occupancy:** Occupancy provides better odds for a favorable outcome, since the borrower likely wants to stay in the home.
- **FMV:** FMV is crucial to determine which category of note to buy at the right price.
- **Title:** Rarely pulled at acquisition on seconds because it's normally done at origination, title is usually not a big risk because it's usually covered contractually in the note sale agreement for lien position and validity from most sellers.
- **Taxes and insurance:** These aren't much of a monitored risk for junior liens because they are usually escrowed and paid for by the senior lien.

Depending on the type of asset and class, investors will eventually start to know what data points are relevant to them and their business model. The best advice I can give to a new note buyer about due diligence is to track your data over time. The information collected going forward about the performance of the assets an investor has purchased will prove invaluable when making future trades. This information will obviously be different for everyone, which is why it's so important to learn from your own trades to see how successful your due diligence proved to be and to make adjustments accordingly. After all, note buying is a very statistical business. This is why you'll see some newer investors buying multiple asset classes of various liens until they determine the data and statistical outcomes for each class in relation to their business model.

CHAPTER 14
TAKEAWAYS

Vetting the seller. Note sellers run the gamut from unprofessional to impeccable. Know whom you're buying from.

Performing versus nonperforming notes: Here's what matters. Borrower's pay history, credit, equity, and geography are all important to consider for performing notes. For nonperforming notes, know the value, the property, the borrower's intent, and the potential exits.

Due diligence for first mortgages (senior liens). This may include value; title and occupancy; taxes, insurance, multiple liens, and HOA fees; as well as location, comparables, and property condition.

Due diligence on second mortgages (junior liens). Is the property high equity or no equity? If the latter, consider the senior lien status, occupancy, fair market value, title, and taxes and insurance.

CHAPTER 15
Exit Strategies

This is the real nitty-gritty—what every prospective NPN buyer wants to learn. NPN collection is a different world from what it was when we started in the business. The creation of the CFPB (Consumer Financial Protection Bureau) and passing of Dodd-Frank created a series of checks and balances for NPN buyers to adhere to. This made us reevaluate our business and loss mitigation practices at PPR. It was a lengthy and expensive process involving licensing, consultants, and a lot of attorney bills. Today, I'm glad we did it because this compliance has made us better note owners, set us apart from our competition, and made us more reliable in the eyes of banks and large note sellers. For anyone planning on pursuing the NPN business, become a licensed servicer or work directly with a licensed servicer.

That being said, the NPN space is still a viable one. There are many ways to profit with NPNs. Depending on the borrower's intent—as well as a note investor's goals, cost of capital, and experience level—the exit chosen can greatly affect how much profit an investor stands to gain. If an investor is not planning on selling the note, there are typically two ways to exit: through the property or through communication with the borrower.

Option 1: Exiting through the Property
When exiting through the property, an investor faces either an adversarial situation through the legal process of foreclosure or more cooperative scenarios involving a deed in lieu of foreclosure or a short sale type of transaction. Exiting through the property could happen

with both first and second nonperforming mortgages. Most re-performing notes, however, whether firsts or seconds, are created when a note owner agrees to a mutually beneficial solution with the borrower. From a strategic standpoint, some investors may prefer to exit through the property to obtain the hard real estate, which is accomplished more often with vacant properties.

Deed in Lieu of Foreclosure

In occupied properties, a common exit strategy involves obtaining a deed in lieu of foreclosure (DIL). If the homeowner cannot afford to stay in the property, a note owner can offer to pay an administration fee, often referred to as cash for keys, while the homeowner signs over the deed in lieu of foreclosure. This strategy could save the homeowner from damaging his or her credit. Some of the benefits to the investor include saving a few thousand dollars in foreclosure fees and costs, saving an average of fifteen months in time depending on which state the property is located in, and reducing the risk of further damage to the property during the legal process.

We bought a mortgage back in March 2016 for $25,000. The property had an as-is FMV of $45,000. It took us about a week to contact the borrower. It was owned by a middle-aged man who couldn't afford to make a payment. He liked the idea of completing a deed-in-lieu to avoid a foreclosure. We asked a Realtor to visit the house to take a look inside and make sure we would be able to easily sell the property. It took a few days for our attorney to draft the DIL, at a cost of $250. The borrower signed the DIL and moved out two weeks later. The Realtor suggested that the property had an ARV of $59,000. We had the trash cleaned out, rekeyed the locks, and cut the grass for a total of $2,300. On the inside we decided to paint and carpet three bedrooms and replace the vinyl floor in the kitchen and bathroom, at a total cost of $6,000. We listed the property in early June for $59,900. We sold the house in late August for $54,750. After sales costs of $3,300, our net profit was approximately $17,900.

Foreclosure and REO

Another option involves foreclosure, which occurs when the note owner reclaims the property, at which point it is considered to be an REO. When a homeowner is unable to make full principal and interest payments on his or her mortgage, the lender can exercise his or her rights to protect his or her interests through the foreclosure and ejectment process.

Taking place after the foreclosure, ejectment is the action to redeem possession of the property, ordering the borrower to vacate the premises after the lender gains title to the collateral through the sheriff's deed. This is now known as an REO. The note owner can then resell the property as is, rent it out, fix it up, and flip it or offer owner financing to recoup as much money as possible. Even after foreclosure, the former note owner/now property owner can still create a plan with the original borrower in some cases (for example, reversing the foreclosure, selling back the property as a lease-to-own, etc.). It's important to mention that an REO isn't a factor of only the note business—it's also an industry in and of itself with its own marketplace and business models specific to this type of real estate.

Option 2: Exiting through the Borrower

In many cases, the note owner's exit is dependent on the borrower—*not* the note owner—because the outcome is usually contingent on the borrower's intent and ability (affordability) and willingness to pay. It's important to keep in mind that, unlike the bank, which originated the loan, the note owner purchased the note at a discount, giving him or her flexibility to offer the homeowner the best option that suits the needs of both parties.

There are many different exit options when dealing with (and exiting through) a borrower with a delinquent mortgage, including:

- **Discounted loan payoff.** In this case, a note investor will accept less than the full payoff remaining on the loan. For example, a note owner can offer a homeowner an opportunity to pay off the loan without incurring additional late fees and penalties. If a note investor paid $20,000 for a second mortgage with a face value of $50,000, for example, he or she could contact the borrower by mail and make an offer like "If you pay $30,000 in the next 60 days, the loan will be considered paid in full." Some homeowners can access this type of capital from their 401(k) while in foreclosure, often without penalty, making this course of action a viable option for them.
- **Reinstating the loan.** The delinquent loan is considered reinstated

when the amount of money needed to bring the past-due loan current has been paid. The term for this past-due amount of money is arrears, which can consist of missed payments, interest fees, late fees, and corporate advances (e.g., back taxes, HOA fees, legal fees, etc.). Sometimes a note owner can accept a partial reinstatement or a discounted arrears plan and put it into action with the homeowner.

- **Payment plan.** Sometimes called a loan modification, there is no one-size-fits-all payment plan for borrowers. Every loan is different, as is every borrower, making for different combinations of arrears and monthly payment options. A typical situation utilizing this strategy is a payment-plus-arrears plan, which would typically spread the reinstatement amount over a defined number of months, along with the regular or reduced payment.

- **Refinance.** Another type of plan instituted with a borrower includes a full or partial reinstatement and regular or reduced payments with the goal of refinancing. This option could take up to twelve months of re-performance and usually requires sufficient equity in the property.

- **Seller assistance.** If the borrower can't afford to stay in the property, the note owner can assist him or her by helping to pay for a Realtor, a mover, a down payment, or rent for a new place. The note owner can also allow the borrower to stay in the current property and buy him or her some time until the property sells. A note owner could even pay the homeowner a commission if a buyer or tenant is found for the property.

Example of a Modified Payment Plan

For example, I bought a HELOC for $19,610 in June 2015. The original note was $200,000, and the unpaid principal balance (UPB) was $195,033, with a payoff of $241,051. The variable interest rate was 3.25 percent. The loan term was 180 months. The arrears owed was $46,016. The FMV was $299,000, and the senior lien was $231,571. So it was a partial-equity second mortgage.

After purchasing the note, we tried multiple times to contact the homeowner, with no success. Next we sent a demand letter, and again, there was no response. The foreclosure complaint was filed soon after the demand letter expired, and a week later, the borrower called. He had filed bankruptcy a few years ago and thought he was no longer obligated to pay back the money. What had happened was, the borrower owned a business that struggled for a few years, but it had turned around since then.

The borrower originally offered $60,000 to satisfy the loan. We declined without a counteroffer, and his next offer was $90,000. Our counter was $165,000, which was higher than he was willing to pay, so he stopped communicating with us. The foreclosure process continued, and when the sale date was set two months later, the borrower called again. He said he needed about a year to exit another business and was willing to pay $120,000 in twelve months to stop the foreclosure. We weren't going to stop and didn't want to risk waiting a year to be paid.

Here's the hybrid solution we agreed to: He paid $5,000 in arrears to stop the foreclosure. We amortized $150,000 for thirty years at 3.25 percent, with a deferred balance of $60,000. The monthly payment was $652.81/month. We added a clause that allowed him to pay off the loan anytime within the following twenty-four months for $130,000, as long as he was current with the monthly payment. If he pays it off within two years, he doesn't have to pay the deferred balance and saves almost $15,000 off the UPB.

Exiting Through Refinancing

In an example from our portfolio, the original note value of a property in Carmel, Indiana, was $14,000, and we paid $4,439 to purchase the re-performing asset in April 2014 from an affiliate, whose current total payoff was $13,600. The real estate market had begun to stabilize in many areas, including Indiana, so more payoff requests were coming in. The total payoff at the time of this borrower's request because of refinancing her home was $11,701.36. The fair market value was $137,900, the senior lien was only $70,566, and her previously modified monthly payment was $295.95 for seventy-nine months. The refinance took place in August 2016, and we collected $4,439.25 plus our payoff of $11,701.36, totaling $16,140.61 on our initial $4,439 investment. Not bad for a two-year investment. Because of the early payoff, our yield went up significantly. Otherwise, we would have received $3,551.40/year in principal and interest payments for six more years, totaling $21,308.40.

Utilizing a Servicer

Upon purchasing a performing note or after modifying a nonperforming note to re-performing status, an investor should keep in mind that there is some minor financial work involved going forward. Payments from each note need to be tracked, delinquent payments that may arise need to be addressed, and all the related accounting needs to be done correctly. A licensed servicer should handle these tasks in order to maintain compliance and accuracy.

Hiring a servicer is similar to a real estate investor or landlord hiring a property manager to manage his or her properties. Instead of property maintenance and tenant management, a note servicer is responsible for all the maintenance and management of a note or note portfolio. When placing a loan with a servicer, a low setup fee is typically required, along with a modest monthly rate. Unlike property management, with fees that can run anywhere from 8–10 percent of gross rent, the flat fee paid to the servicer every month is the same whether the note payments are $300/month or $3,000/month.

The reason for the drastic rate difference between property management and mortgage servicing is that the latter is much more automated and scalable. So unlike property managers, note servicers don't have to be local, and they don't have to deal with as many tenants or turnover issues, since borrowers usually have a vested interest, especially when it comes to staying in their primary residence. It's also important to note that in nearly all cases, the cost of hiring a servicer (who can work in multiple states) will be covered by the monthly payments being earned from the note.

The biggest benefit of hiring a servicer is that it makes performing notes completely passive for a buy-and-hold investor. So with all the accounting and collections taken care of, there really isn't much for investors to do other than head out to the mailbox to collect their checks and hand their monthly statements to their accountant.

CHAPTER 15
TAKEAWAYS

Where's the exit? You typically have two options with nonperforming notes: exiting through the property (deed in lieu of foreclosure, foreclosure and REO) and exiting through the borrower (discounted loan payoff, reinstating the loan, payment plan, refinance, seller assist).

Why use servicers? Note owners using note servicers can be analogous to real estate owners using property managers. Yes, they add some expense, but they handle almost all the routine work associated with owning a note.

CHAPTER 16
Recapitalization

When our business really began, after our first few notes, we decided to raise some private money and buy more product. As we worked through more notes, we learned that by turning nonperforming notes into re-performing notes through a modification with the borrower, a note owner not only increases a note's value but can also make a substantial profit along the way. As a note owner, we could collect arrears payments as well. Overall, we were achieving better results than we did our first time around and were starting to track the data. The only problem was, by the time we were done working through many of the assets, we realized we weren't recapitalizing fast enough! The cash flow was great, but we were really just waiting for monthly payments to come in. And I know you're probably thinking, Why not just sell the notes? Well, the answer lies in two reasons.

For one, these notes were newly re-performing, so they needed "seasoning" of at least a few months to make sure the borrower was comfortable with the new payment plan. Some investors have the model of modifying NPNs to performing status and then collecting a set number of monthly payments to season the notes while they determine whether the borrower's payment plan will be effective for the future (and for any future note buyers). This seasoning generates a return for them while also increasing the note's value by demonstrating that the note is consistently performing and the borrower is reliably making payments.

The other reason: We couldn't simply sell these notes right away because there was very little demand or marketplace for junior liens at that time. So again, we had to get creative. Without much of a market for junior liens, we had to try to create one. The best way to do that, we figured, was through education, a lesson we had learned from our previous lives as private capital fund-raisers. We built an education platform to teach the junior lien space with courses, conference calls, and speaking events. We traveled to real estate groups and eventually migrated our education platform online. Today we no longer educate in this way because of compliance and a shifting business model, but it really helped us get off the ground and build a database of note buyers. Today this list is in the tens of thousands and growing. What we learned from this time was that to really grow, we had to speed up the model of modifying nonperforming loans with a few different recapitalization strategies.

The Key to Speeding Up Cash Flow: Velocity

The initial goal for most new note investors is to build a steady portfolio of performing notes, whether they purchased them while performing or rehabilitated a note back to re-performing status. Then they just "sit back" and collect the payments. This business model is very similar to investing in rental properties or any long-term buy-and-holds. It offers the opportunity to continue building wealth over time, especially when the cash flow from the notes enables the purchase of additional notes. This was our goal initially, too, and is still part of our business model today. But if you want to truly grow a note company or build substantial wealth in the note business, you have to implement the idea of velocity. Recapitalize sooner rather than later. Investors can implement a velocity model by either selling or flipping the note, selling a partial note, or creating a collateral assignment of note and mortgage.

Recapitalization Method No. 1: Selling the Note

Since a note is an asset, it can always be sold, whether re-performing or nonperforming. You can find note buyers almost anywhere; some of the best places to start are local REIA meetings or real estate and note meet-up groups. Many buyers can be found online through websites like FCI Exchange, LoanMLS, BiggerPockets, and a variety of LinkedIn groups. When we started our business, not all these platforms existed or provided a way to sell notes, so this wasn't an instant option for us. Either way, from selling notes in a variety of ways over the years, we learned the best note buyer is the one who's already a customer. Repeat quality service is best. Some other great ways to proactively continue sales include providing reps and warrants with notes to give buyers more security and offering them quality collateral and follow-up service. We also found that offering a "performance" warranty was another huge selling point to our note buyers. It took the biggest objection—"What if my re-performing note goes non-performing again?"—off the table. And with quality loss mitigation practices, we found that the amount of these re-performing loans that fall into delinquent status tends to be a small percentage of our overall portfolio.

Recapitalization Method No. 2: Flipping the Note

Another method of selling the note is to flip it, which simply means buying it for one price and selling it for a higher price. If an investor were to go through the work of purchasing a nonperforming note or notes wholesale, he or she can then sell it at a retail value as is or proceed to modify it. This can sometimes work with re-performing notes, too, and again brings up the concept of seasoning because, up to a certain point, the longer a note investor holds on to a re-performing note, especially after a recent modification, the more likely it will rise in value, since many risk-averse note buyers are looking for a note that has a longer pay history. If an investor buys a low-equity or no-equity note, he or she could also wait for some equity to come back into the marketplace and then flip the note out for a higher price.

Recapitalization Method No. 3: Selling a Partial Note

I was first exposed to the idea of partials in the seller-financed note world. I'm not sure this strategy was used often in the institutional world, since prior to PPR and the rise of the junior lien market, I think the majority of institutional note investors didn't have a need to bring this strategy into their portfolio because they were dealing with larger first mortgages with more capital at their disposal. Still, this can be another recapitalization strategy that allows note owners to sell part of their note to an investor where the amount, term, and interest rate may align with exactly what they want in a note and can afford. For example, with a fifteen-year note, if one investor didn't have the available capital or preferred a note with a shorter term, he or she could purchase the first ten years of monthly payments from a current note owner. By doing so, the current note owner would reclaim his or her initial note investment while remaining entitled to the last five years of payments. This option can benefit both the partial note investor and the note owner.

Benefits for the Investor Buying the Partial

- Partial notes limit the amount of money invested because they require only a portion of the total cost of the note.
- Because partial notes contain only a portion of payments, the term for the investor is shorter, and his or her capital returns in a much shorter time span.
- In the event of a foreclosure, the new investor is the first to get paid.

Benefits for the Note Owner Selling the Partial

- A note owner will regain a portion of his or her initial investment capital after a partial note is sold, leaving him or her with less risk in that particular note. That capital can then be reinvested in another opportunity.
- If interest rates rise in the future, a shorter period of full ownership will reduce inflationary risk.
- The overall risk is cut in half because the investor and note seller share the risk of the note together.
- If a note owner had a note that wasn't fully covered by equity, he or she could still sell a partial or the portion of the note that *was* backed by equity.

Recapitalization Method No. 4:
Collateral Assignment of Note and Mortgage

While we were waiting for the junior lien marketplace to catch up with us and fine-tuning our methods and reach with our junior lien education, we still needed capital. This is where the revolutionary concept of a collateral assignment of note and mortgage came in. Collateral assignments, as they're often simply called, let note owners borrow money from an investor and use their note as collateral (once again capitalizing on the idea of leverage). Very similar to a car loan, in which the car acts as collateral for the loan, a collateral assignment is done by using a promissory note between a note owner and his or her new investor, spelling out the terms and the interest rate on the new loan.

The recording of the collateral assignment in the county where the property behind the note is located perfects, or permanently attaches, the collateral that's being used to protect the new lender. The velocity factor comes in when the note owner uses this borrowed capital to purchase more notes, again utilizing leverage, creating exponential growth. Also, it's a great way to recapitalize tax-free because it's a loan, just like a real estate investor refinancing a rental property.

Borrowing Private Money Utilizing Collateral Assignments

It was this exact type of leverage that we used to build PPR, especially in the beginning, when we needed capital the most. Finding buyers fast enough for all of our product was obviously a challenge, and raising enough capital privately was still tough because we were so new in our business. So when we discovered collateral assignments, we found a way to solve both of our problems.

Using our previous private money contacts in the real estate industry, we came up with the solution: borrow against our notes that had equity, creating new private notes with hard or private money investors. We would then use these performing notes as the collateral for our new private loans, purchasing new notes with tax-free capital. Now we were moving and reinvesting private equity much as a bank leverages depositors' money, creating both a profitable recapitalization strategy and a source of capital to buy more notes. This got us through the rougher start-up times until we were able to build a more sustainable business model to raise private money from investors and had a means to sell enough of our notes to note buyers.

CHAPTER 16
TAKEAWAYS

Key concept: the velocity of capital. "Turning" capital faster can often be better, especially if you're not a buy-and-hold investor and you're looking for growth.

Ways to recapitalize after buying a note. Note investors have several good options for recapitalizing as needed: They can sell/flip the whole note, sell a partial note, or do a collateral assignment.

CHAPTER 17

Sources of Capital and Getting Started in Notes

Not everyone has a portfolio of assets to start utilizing collateral assignments, and even if they do, they may not have a network of private money investors willing to lend money against a note. Note buyers looking to purchase a performing note that has equity, current senior lien status (in the case of buying a second lien), significant pay history, or other desirable qualities need to understand that these conditions come at a price. These elements can make notes a capital-intensive business. But the source really depends on the investors, their financial situation, and what they would like to do in the note business. I often talk about the benefits of leverage and using private money because, as with any business, learning how to find or effectively raise capital can be the best way to grow exponentially. But that isn't always necessary for everyone. In fact, here are a few examples outside savings, personal capital, and asset liquidation in which an investor wouldn't need to use leverage for his or her source of capital:

- **Retirement funds.** I meet many investors who aren't aware that they can use retirement capital for notes. Self-directed accounts such as IRAs, education savings accounts (ESAs), health savings accounts (HSAs), and even 401(k)s can provide another resource for capital. Many investors who hold a day job or have earned income of some kind have paid into a 401(k) for a number of years and built up quite a balance. In many cases, money from accounts like these can be used to purchase notes. Each retirement account is different, and it is important to understand the rules governing any such fund. This is especially the case with any self-directed accounts.

- **Home equity loans.** Similar to a traditional mortgage, but usually with a shorter term and a higher rate, home equity loans generally come in two varieties. One is usually for a fixed term and fixed payment, and the other takes the form of a HELOC with a variable rate and a fixed draw period. Home equity loans and lines of credit are both loans that use the equity in a home as collateral for additional leverage. In previous stories, I talked about the inherent risks that come along with HELOCs (especially on your primary residence), so it's important to be cognizant of that when using them in relation to your note portfolio.

- **Partnerships.** Although most investors start by simply purchasing one or two notes, others want to progress rapidly and begin buying larger ones. After all, that is another way to get wholesale prices. In this case, an investor must start a partnership. A partnership consists of a group of investors getting together, pooling their money, and creating a partnership agreement. A group of investors can also start a private placement and collect money from people outside themselves to purchase notes or combine outside capital with their own funds. The greatest benefit to the partnership is that investors will have increased buying power, better pricing, and economies of scale, all while deploying a limited amount of their own capital. Alongside utilizing collateral assignments, we used this strategy simultaneously to purchase notes in the beginning, and we still do it today.

Now you're ready to get out there and go buy some notes! Before I conclude this book and tell you how to get started in the note business, I want to leave you with two examples of what I think is one of the most powerful concepts of note investing. This is something that I learned from the bank and throughout my career in relation to harnessing the power of leverage. And it may be my favorite thing about notes: Institutional notes can be used to pay your debts. This is something I started to toy with a few years after starting PPR and working in the notes business. Obviously I'm a fan of buying intentionally, but as I've gotten closer to retirement age, I think this concept also comes from purposeful planning. Like all my strategies and concepts, it's easiest for me to describe by example.

College for a Fraction of the Cost

Think back to your first note. For some people, it was their car loan or their mortgage. My first note was my student loan, as I explained in the first section of the book. It was the same for my son—only when he got to college age, I had already started in the note business and figured out that if we were to employ two different investing strategies together, we could pay for his college tuition with a fraction of the money. So instead of my wife and me just writing a check, my son took out a student loan and my wife also took out a student loan. The main reason we did this was not just that student loan interest can be deductible but that if we could use the borrowed money (at approximately 6–7 percent) to pay for tuition and our money stayed invested (at approximately 12–18 percent), making a substantially higher yield, that alone would offset the cost of his tuition. But it gets better.

For some loans, you don't have to make payments right away, and some even have deferral periods, like six months after graduation, usually put in place so the student can find a job by that time. This gave us even more time and money to earn more arbitrage money. The second part of the strategy has to do with the timing. Right before payments on the student loan were coming due, we purchased a re-performing note with a similar monthly payment and a term that had a longer time frame than the student loan. We purchased this note for a significant discount. Keep in mind, a re-performing second lien can be purchased for anywhere from 40–60 percent of the payoff, and now the payment we receive from the note can be used to pay the student loan payment. It still pays us even today! So we paid for roughly $100,000 worth of college tuition with just under $40,000! Pretty powerful stuff, but that's not all this concept can do.

Free or Low-Cost Insurance

Along the same line of thinking, this strategy of having your assets pay your liabilities was first introduced to me by a builder whom I worked for way back before I became a real estate investor. This happened when I was twenty years old, still in college. He introduced me to what's known as the infinite banking concept. Here's how it worked: When he borrowed the money to build a house, he would do it out of his life insurance policy instead of going to a traditional bank for a construction loan. He'd then sell the house for a nice profit (usually for at least a $75,000 to $100,000 gain) and pay back the insurance policy with that capital, even overfunding the policy when possible. And for his next house, he would just rinse and repeat this process over and over again.

Later on, when I got into the institutional note business, I would show some of my note buyers and fund investors how they could get free or low-cost insurance by employing this same strategy. And it's pretty simple. Overfund your permanent life insurance policy, borrow the money out to buy a note (at 4–5 percent interest on the loan from the policy), proceed to buy a performing note with a 10–18 percent return, and use the spread, or arbitrage, to go toward the loan payments, interest, and premium payments. And there you have it—notes will buy you "free" or at least very low cost insurance.

Getting "free" insurance or paying for college at a fraction of the cost is really just the tip of the iceberg in terms of what you can do with notes. What I love more than anything about explaining these strategies is when investors come back to me with new spins on the same idea. Before you get started in the note business, it's important to be thinking, Are there things in my life that I can pay for with note investing?

How to Get Started in the Note Business

When a note investor finds himself or herself at the final step in this note cycle, what he or she has actually done is arrived at the beginning again: finding capital for the next purchase to start the whole process over. The only difference is that hopefully this time around, he or she will start with more affordable capital, a reliable source of product, and better data to make a more profitable trade—and, if the investor is in NPN world, knowledge of the workout or loan modification process to create superior deals for both himself or herself as well as the borrower. Oh, and the willingness to go through that cycle all over again!

When we fast-forward several years from our little money-raising problem to where PPR is today, we're at a much different place. Now we're working *on* our business instead of just *in* it; we have far surpassed my initial goal when starting the company of owning one hundred notes. But not everyone is able to or even interested in going through our exact journey, nor should they be. As with any industry, there is no one-size-fits-all way to become successful with notes. It all comes down to where you would like to be in the industry.

What Kind of Investor Are You?

Before starting to search for available notes to purchase, it's important for an investor to ask, Where do I see myself in the note business?

As with real estate and other types of debt investing, notes offer limitless possibilities for investors. Sometimes these possibilities reveal themselves while you're working in other aspects of the industry, but to start to determine this niche, it's a good idea to visualize an endgame. This endgame could be starting a business, becoming a part-time investor, making retirement money, or simply supplementing income. When it comes to choosing a note niche, it is helpful to start by evaluating risk tolerance, knowledge level, time commitment, and available capital to deploy. The two most direct ways to get started in institutional notes are through fund investing and/or note buying.

Fund Investing

The simplest way for many investors to get into notes is through a note fund. This is where a company or a group of investors attempt to diversify their risk by combining their money together into a fund to buy a tape or pool of mortgages. An investor can passively invest capital with one of these funds and expect recurring cash flow in the form of a preferred return. Although some funds allow unaccredited investors, the majority accept capital solely from those who are accredited. Currently, accredited investors are those who meet the criteria of income of $200,000/year if single or $300,000/year if married or who have $1 million in net assets, not counting their primary residence.

Some note funds may also allow up to thirty-five unaccredited "sophisticated" investors. For more detailed information on the full SEC regulations, consult www.sec.gov. Fund investing offers limited time commitment and liability, as well as fewer constraints on how much capital can be deployed, often with a comparable return to performing notes.

Buying Notes

For those who are unaccredited or wish to invest in multiple options, investors can also, of course, purchase nonperforming and/or performing notes. Performing note buyers generally need more capital to purchase notes but much less expertise and time to own and maintain their portfolio versus nonperforming note buyers. With either option, investors can "become the bank," utilizing high-yield assets, secured by real estate.

So whether you're a high–net worth individual who is looking for mailbox money from a note fund or a more hands-on investor looking to use leverage to build a portfolio of passive cash-flowing assets, notes are an alternative investment that offer a clear path toward financial freedom.

CHAPTER 17
TAKEAWAYS

How to get capital for notes? Whether from your own money, retirement income, or partnerships or through OPM, there are many ways to find the capital for investing in notes.

Paying debt with notes. Notes can be used for everything from offsetting college costs to obtaining "free" or low-cost insurance.

How to get started in the note business. Determine what kind of note investor you want to be, then use fund investing or note investing via purchasing notes to get started.

CHAPTER 18

What I Would Do Differently Today as a Real Estate Investor

Although I'm truly grateful for everything I've learned and all the fabulous people I've met, and really all the success I've had from real estate investing and notes over the years, there are also many things I would probably do differently if I could do it all over again. When I look back at what has happened over the course of my own football game of life (ages twenty-five to sixty-five—though I'm not quite at the finish line yet!), I can't help going back to the very beginning. All those aha moments are the ones I tend to think about the most. It's not so much that I would change these moments or how I got there; it's really a matter of speeding things up and doing more sooner.

The first one that comes to mind was from all those years ago, before I even walked into that DIG meeting. All those times when I was considering doing some networking or going to a meeting and didn't. I wish I could just say to that guy, *"Do it!* Don't wait. Go now." I always thought I was too busy to go to a meeting. I felt as if I couldn't afford to spend the time there, that I had too much work to do. Well, now I know, with all the opportunities that have opened up to me because of those meetings, I couldn't afford *not* to do them! Joining think tanks, attending business leader meetings, and enlisting the help of coaches and consultants has helped our business grow only better and faster. Because of this outside help, PPR was able to go from a club of three guys working from home to what I believe to be an enduring enterprise for years to come.

Outside personal development and networking, there are many other strategies (even ones I've outlined in previous chapters) that I could have employed better or differently to intentionally build and preserve more wealth sooner. And if I had to do it all over again, it would hopefully be with more efficiency and less aggravation. So if you were me, at any point in this book, perhaps the following will apply to you and help you get to where you're going sooner and better.

My Do-over

Sure, budgeting while working a second job and living well below my means were ways I could save money to build my investing nest egg... but could I have done better? Smarter? A new saying, or at least new to me, that I like is "Make more, save less." Reserves are critical, as are budgeting and saving. You can't get started successfully in investing without it, but I could have started my journey with less suffering (though it definitely built character!). It took me running out of my own hard-earned capital to get creative, but once I did, with the idea of using unsecured debt to buy houses, it changed everything. The use of OPM was my first taste of leverage, and I couldn't get enough. Later utilizing HELOCs and, eventually, private and hard money changed my investing forever. If I were starting over again, I could only hope to discover it all sooner. I could do all the deals I wanted! It even led me to get creative with my deals later on, raising private money myself, and the rest, as they say, is history.

From my time at DIG and my work as a mentor, I've come to learn that it's pivotal to get educated in your niche, network with others doing it, and enlist a mentor or coach with more experience if possible. And if you really want to do something big, get free. Like many other business leaders I meet in the real estate space, we all managed to find financial freedom through traditional real estate before taking the giant leap to bigger endeavors. This doesn't mean be retired; what I really mean is get free from your 9-5 with real estate if you really want to be able to take bigger risks.

When I really think about this so-called do-over, I start to evaluate my wealth today and where it came from. Outside my work at PPR, I've determined that much of my real wealth as an investor has come from the following four main things. I wish I had known these concepts when starting out:

No. 1. Money saved on taxes. Wouldn't it be nice to have some or even all the money you pay in taxes to use for investments? The IRS rewards us with tax breaks for providing housing, jobs, and charity, so shouldn't we build our strategies around obtaining as many of those rewards as we can? I was fortunate enough to learn this relatively early on as a student of accounting and as a Realtor, but I still wouldn't mind getting some of that tax money back from when I had my own small business! So connect with an investor-friendly accountant sooner.

No. 2. Investing intentionally. This means with purpose, goals, and exit strategies in mind. Though I did this with many of my owner-occupied houses, I wish I had done this more with the houses I sold to investors as an investor-friendly Realtor, as well as my commercial endeavors. And of course in my note business, we just jumped right in without anywhere to turn. In the beginning, that blind ignorance was a bit of a blessing in disguise, since we didn't realize what we were fully embarking on. But I also know that if our intentions had been clearer in those early years, with a defined direction for the company, we would have been where we are today much sooner. Be intentional!

No. 3. Leverage. Whether leveraging money, people, time, or technology, this is key to being a successful investor. Partner that with the use of compound interest and other banking concepts, and you're ready to be the bank. I focused too much on sticks and bricks while I was in accumulation mode. Being stuck in the world of commissions and managing properties, I was distracted by the one thing that creates wealth quickest. Make leverage work for you!

No. 4. Purposeful planning. This goes beyond the intentional investing concept. This is a long-term strategy and how your investments relate to your business. Without realizing it, I created synergy between hard real estate and notes. This can be done for anyone with various pillars of wealth building, whether they're businesses, real estate, notes, or other investments. Then beyond that, it's about how this synergy plays into your long-term goals and the future of your wealth (think estate planning, legacy planning, retirement, taxes, and family governance). All things to be cognizant of and things I wish I'd considered with all my investments. Plan purposefully!

As investors, I think all of us have one ultimate financial goal, and that is to be earning as much passive income as possible by retirement age at the latest. And doing so as fast as possible and as early as possible makes it all the better. It's beyond the financial freedom that gets you out of the rat race; it's long-term wealth for you and your loved ones. I think if I had employed all four of the above into my strategy and life from day one, I could have saved myself a lifetime of mistakes while obtaining the ultimate amount of passive income.

My Philosophy

My son always tells me he has to stop listening whenever I start talking about "my philosophy," but I promised him I'd keep it brief. If I had to sum it up, I'd have to say my biggest regret with investing is not thinking big enough soon enough. I was used to being the poor kid from the suburbs on the outskirts of Philadelphia. I was always too focused on commission, rentals, individual notes. I was stepping over dollars to pick up dimes. I even had the knowledge right in front of me! I provided all the pieces for my fellow investors to get rich in a big way and didn't take enough of my own advice.

It reminds me of the old saying (that I'm paraphrasing) about not trying to make the right decisions all the time but more about *making the decision right*. Be comfortable in your investment decision, and be willing to course-correct if everything doesn't go right or as planned. Nothing is foolproof, and nothing is 100 percent. That's definitely a major takeaway from my stories. The important thing is to not be afraid of failure and to trust yourself enough to know that even if things go wrong, you can still come out on the other side. If we had been afraid of failure after the two notes we got wiped on, we probably wouldn't have our business today. Or if I had accepted the failure of my doomed commercial projects as a sign of my ability to raise private capital, I wouldn't have found notes or even be writing this book. And if I had been afraid to leave my (semi) comfortable job working for someone else as a contractor, I would never have reached entrepreneurial success. Now, of course, I don't mean to say "quit your job now, no matter what the circumstances." What I really mean is to get to the point where you are able to trust your instincts and feel comfortable with necessary risks.

The simplest way to let yourself trust in your own decisions is by getting educated. Do your due diligence, but more important, make sure the timing is right. If you've noticed, most of the strategies in this book depend on timing as well. If there's one constant that I've recognized throughout the past thirty years as an investor, it's that the market and the financing never stay the same. It's a finance-driven business no matter what you do in the real estate world, whether it's hard property or notes. This is why keeping your finger on the pulse and doing things like taking a banker to lunch are so important. Throughout my career, I've been forced to adapt to the market and the available financing, and I've accepted the challenge. I had to. Even today I'm still turned down for traditional financing sometimes because of the amount of mortgages in my own name, but I still try! And sometimes it works, and I get through! These things change; don't be afraid to be persistent while you change along with it.

I keep mentioning this idea of "sooner" or "if I had only known that sooner," and really this all comes back to one thing: knowing yourself. If I had known myself better and had focused on what I was good at and passionate about, I would probably be further along in my journey by now. Whenever investors ask me for one piece of advice (an impossible question), it's hard to say, "Know yourself," so I usually keep it simple: Focus on your strengths, don't let yourself get stuck trying to improve your weaknesses, and think about what type of investor you want to be. Do what you love, and love what you do. See, I'm getting a little too philosophical already! My point is, I'm the *investor that I want to be* today because I did everything in this book. This has really been my investor life story. I can only hope it has shown you the power of what can be achieved when you combine notes and note concepts into your everyday real estate investing and your investing life story.

Glossary

After-repair value (ARV)—The post-repair (potential) value of a property that needs repair or updating. Typically, ARV is estimated when considering the purchase of a property.

Appreciation—The increase of a property's or an asset's fair market value over time. The increase can occur for a variety of reasons that could include increased demand or diminishing supply or an effect of inflation and/or changes in interest rates.

Arbitrage—The practice of taking advantage of a price difference between two or more markets by striking a combination of matching deals that capitalizes on this imbalance, the profit being the difference between market prices. In my case, I applied this to financing by borrowing money via a HELOC at about 4 percent and then lending it out at 12–15 percent, making a nice profit on the difference.

Business line of credit—An arrangement between a lender and a business customer that establishes a maximum loan balance that the lender permits the borrower to access or maintain. This loan is tied to an operating business or entity.

Buy-and-hold property—A property purchased as a long-term investment, usually as a cash-flowing rental property and/or an appreciating asset.

Collateral assignment of note and mortgage—Assigning ownership of a note to a lender as collateral for a loan. I like to do this with private money, where private lenders are assigned a performing loan as collateral for their capital. In other words, their loan to me is backed by a *paper* asset (which is itself backed by a piece of real estate).

Commercial financing—Typically this encompasses private or institutional loans secured by commercial properties such as self-storage facilities, office complexes, etc., but this can also be a commercial blanket loan that can be secured to any kind of property (including residential) or even be unsecured.

Commercial line of credit—Funds made available by a lender to a business to borrow at any given time that the loan docs allow, often for a specified purpose such as real estate acquisition.

Comps (also known as comparables)—Comps are similar properties in proximity to the subject property that are used in underwriting a loan to help determine the value of the subject property.

Compound interest—Interest earned on interest and principal over time.

Conforming loan—A mortgage loan that conforms to a government agency's set of lending guidelines (e.g., Fannie Mae and Freddie Mac programs).

Consumptive debt—Borrowing money to consume, as opposed to borrowing for productive purposes. Credit card debt is an example of consumptive debt, assuming the card was used to purchase consumer goods.

Debt-to-income (DTI) ratio—A measure that expresses an individual's debt load relative to his or her gross income. Debt-to-income ratio, usually expressed as a percentage, is one of the criteria lenders use to establish capacity for new debt.

Delinquent mortgage—A mortgage loan for which the borrower has failed to make payments as agreed. Also known as a nonperforming loan.

Depreciation—The decline in the stated value of an asset over time because of the use and/or age. In effect, this is a tax and accounting matter, not related to the market value of an asset.

Destructive debt (also known as "bad debt")—This is debt that is not used for productive purposes. A typical example would be credit card debt that was acquired to fund lifestyle.

Dodd-Frank—A complex law passed in 2010 that places major regulations on the financial industry, including companies engaged in originating and servicing mortgages. See: http://www.cftc.gov/idc/groups/public/@swaps/documents/file/hr4173_enrolledbill.pdf.

Draw schedule—A schedule or agreement about when incremental funds are released by a lender to the borrower (rehabber) for a construction/renovation/repair project, usually based on the progress of the project.

Due diligence—The research and analysis done by an investor when considering making an investment.

Equity—The difference between the value of an asset and the liabilities on that asset. This is derived from the difference between a property's market value and the amount the owner owes on the property.

FHA financing—A type of government-backed mortgage financing that is known for being borrower friendly. See: https://www.hud.gov/buying/loans.

Forced appreciation—As opposed to market-based appreciation, forced appreciation results from making changes to the economic fundamentals of a property. For example, in a commercial property, you "force" appreciation (increase in value) by increasing revenue through making improvements in the units and raising rents.

Fractional reserve banking—A banking system in which only a portion of deposits is backed by actual cash on hand. The advantage of this system is that it frees up capital for making loans.

Hard money—A short-term loan for the purchase and renovation of a property. Hard money lenders typically charge a higher interest rate than traditional financing, but they can deploy capital faster.

Home equity line of credit (HELOC)—A line of credit available to borrowers to borrow against and use at will (although its deductibility may be limited based on the way they use the funds) with their home equity pledged as collateral. A HELOC typically comes with variable interest rates. A lender can foreclose on the home if payments are not made as agreed.

Home equity loan—A loan granted to a property owner that uses the equity in the property to secure the loan.

Institutional note—A loan originated from a bank or lending institution, as opposed to one created by an individual or private company.

Interchange—A fee charged by banks that covers the cost of handling and credit risk inherent in a bank credit or debit card transaction.

Junior lien—The subordinate to a senior (first) lien based on the recording date.

Lease option—An agreement between a tenant and a landlord that gives a tenant the option to purchase a property during or at the end of the lease term. As long as the lease option period is in effect, the landlord/seller may not offer the property for sale to anyone else. When the term expires, the renter may either exercise or forfeit the purchase option. A lease *option* gives a renter/potential buyer more flexibility than a lease-purchase *agreement*, which requires the renter to purchase the property at the end of the rental period.

Leverage—Using borrowed capital to your advantage to receive a higher return on an investment. In physics, a small force can move a bigger one if a lever is used. In finance, a small amount of liquid capital can combine with borrowed funds to make a larger investment.

Lien—An encumbrance placed on an asset by a lender as security for the loan.

Loan exchange—An online platform used to broker notes for sale or for purchase to/from approved and vetted buyers and sellers.

Loan-to-value (LTV) ratio—The ratio of the amount a lender provides a borrower for a property in relation to its value.

Net interest margin—A measure of the difference between the interest income generated by banks or other financial institutions and the amount of interest paid out to their lenders (e.g., deposits), relative to the amount of their (interest-earning) assets.

Nonperforming note—A loan that a borrower has not made payments on in at least ninety days. Also called a delinquent loan or delinquent note.

Nonrecourse mortgage—A mortgage that doesn't require a borrower to personally sign on the note. In a default, the lender normally cannot pursue any personal assets of the borrower but only the asset that's acting as collateral for the loan.

Note (a.k.a. promissory note)—A contract that is, in effect, a promise to repay a loan.

OPM—An informal acronym that stands for "other people's money." Can be either private or hard money.

Owner financing—A type of financing in which the property owner assists in the financing of his or her own property for the buyer. The seller is basically acting like a bank in this type of transaction.

Performing note—A loan for which a borrower makes payments as agreed on in the terms of their loan.

Phantom appreciation—When a note is purchased at a discount with partial or no equity in a down market and equity returns in an up market, thus increasing value in that asset.

Private mortgage insurance (PMI)—Insurance against default that is required when a borrower makes a down payment of less than 20 percent in a conventional loan.

Private placement memorandum (PPM)—A private offering document that provides information on an investment and the terms that go with it. In this book, we discuss the use of PPMs to raise capital for note funds.

Private equity—Capital typically acquired from high–net worth investors inside a private offering structure or PPM. This capital is typically invested in companies or private funds.

Private money—A loan from a private, noninstitutional source typically to fund a real estate deal. A private money lender could be a friend or a family member or any private individual. IRAs and other retirement accounts can be good sources of private money.

Productive debt (also known as good debt)—Borrowing funds to make investments, as opposed to borrowing to consume or spend on liabilities.

Real estate owned (REO)—Foreclosed properties owned by the bank or lender.

Recapitalization—In Wall Street terms, it's the readjustment of a company's debt in an attempt to stabilize the capital structure. In note investing, recapitalization of a note deal on the part of an individual or company could consist of flipping a note, selling all or part of a note, or borrowing against it.

Re-performing note—A note that had been delinquent but has been worked out or "rehabbed" and is now performing (i.e., the borrower is again paying on it). It could have gone through some form of loan modification based on the borrower's situation or simply been brought back to the original contract after a payment was missed.

Residential financing—A loan used to buy a one- to four-unit residential property.

Roth IRA—An individual retirement account, funded by after-tax dollars, from which gains may be withdrawn after retirement on a tax-free basis. See: https://www.irs.gov/retirement-plans/roth-iras.

Secured note—A loan that has an asset attached to it as collateral. There is decreased risk with secured loans because of the assets backed by the loan; therefore, the interest rate earned by the lender is lower.

Seller assist—When a seller of a property contributes money to cover certain closing costs on the house.

Seller carry (also known as a seller carry-back and seller financing)—Owner-provided financing in the form of a private note. You may also see this advertised as seller financing or "owner will carry" (OWC).

Senior lien (first lien)—The first lien or mortgage tied to a property; recorded before any other lien or mortgage. During foreclosure, the senior lien is settled first.

Servicer—A company that collects interest, principal, and escrow payments from a borrower. It also typically handles accounting and reporting.

Servicing rights—The legal rights to be the servicer of loans.

Single-family residence (SFR)—A stand-alone structure that has no attachment to any other residence. It is usually built on a lot that is larger than the structure, which creates a yard surrounding the home. It is the opposite of a multifamily residence.

Stepped-up basis—The readjustment of the value of an appreciated asset like a property for tax purposes upon inheritance, determined to be the presumably higher market value of the asset at the time of inheritance. In other words, the heir isn't required to pay taxes on the gain in value that the deceased owner experienced with the property.

Subject-to—Buying a property subject to an existing mortgage that you (the new buyer) continue making payments on. The original bank financing stays in place after ownership is transferred from the borrower to a new buyer.

Trade desk—A sales platform that can be online and is used to facilitate the sale (and sometimes the purchase) of notes. Many trade desks are in-house for banks and specialty servicers, while some smaller community banks and individual note sellers utilize loan exchanges.

Transactional funding—Extremely short term funding used to enable a buyer to purchase a property, typically as part of a "double closing" in which an investor is buying and then immediately reselling a property.

Unsecured note—A loan with no asset attached, which may increase the risk for a lender in the event of a default.

Usury laws—Government regulation on loan interest rates. These laws are intended to protect consumers from being charged unreasonably high rates. Usury laws do not apply to commercial loans.

Wraparound land contract—The seller, who owns a property that has a mortgage, lends a buyer the difference between the seller's existing loan amount and the purchase price, thereby "wrapping" the existing loan in a new loan that includes both. The buyer's periodic loan payments are sufficient to repay the preexisting loan as well as the seller's "wrap" loan.

Acknowledgments

It's really just incredible the number of people I've met and experiences I've had throughout my life and career. All of them make me appreciative of their influence and have encouraged me to continue to share strategies to help others to share, build, and preserve their wealth over the years. But let's get specific. First and foremost, I have to thank those who made this book possible: Josh Dorkin and the incredible team at BiggerPockets, including Brandon Turner, Katie Askew, and Scott Trench. Also thank you to my editing and design team: Taylor Hugo, Paul Silverman, Katelin Hill, Jarrod Jemison, and Wendy Dunning. It was BiggerPockets that not only gave me a platform for my writing but also recognized it as something worthwhile enough to create this book.

Next, I'm charged with the monumental task of trying to thank all the folks who influenced me over the years. My mentors: starting with my uncle Ray Van Horn for being my moral compass, Tony Liberati, my construction dad, Mike Carr of Carr Real Estate (my first brokerage), Pat Tiehel at Long & Foster Real Estate (my brokerage for the past ten years), to my modern coaches, Marc Sinkow, Cheryl Beth Kuchler, and Lewis Schiff. And let's not forget my instructor from my real estate investor class who first introduced me to OPM (or "other people's money"), Dominick. I've also been blessed with the greatest network ever known to most real estate investors. Besides the online network of BiggerPockets, I've had the great fortune of my local national REIA group (DIG), as well as the years with fellow organizations I've enjoyed founding and running: RING (Real Estate Investor Networking Group), SIA (Strategic Investor Alliance), and now the Mid-Atlantic Real Estate Investor Summit.

But now it's time to thank those who really inspired me to give back to the community. Mr. Steve Babiak, my friend and DIG colleague, comes to mind first, seeing as he was the very first person who ever mentioned BiggerPockets to me and piqued my interest in this new way of connecting with investors. Then, of course, there's my work family, who helped make this all happen and continue to help people all over the country, from investors to homeowners: my Partners at PPR, John Sweeney and Bob Paulus, as well my wonderful marketing and investor relations team, Tiffany Zerby, Peter Neill, Tom McCarthy, and, of course, the rest of the PPR team who keep the lights on. Also, Scott Corbett and his marketing group at Lightmark Media, whose invaluable input enabled all of this to come together.

And last but not least, there's whom I do all of this for, my family. My son Chris, who has continually persuaded me to tell my stories and give advice throughout the BiggerPockets site. Being the writer in the family, he's someone who's been instrumental in editing and developing my storytelling skills both on the blog and in the book; without his help, this book would not have happened. Then there's the rest of my family: my darling wife, Shirl, my other favorite son, Brendon, and my mother, Kathleen, who has always encouraged me to help others and tell my story. Finally, my beautiful grandkids: Tyler, Gianna, and Beckham, whom I want to leave these concepts to the most. It's with great joy I get to share with you all my greatest strategies, and with the help of this book, I hope to continue doing so for many years to come.

More from
BiggerPockets Publishing

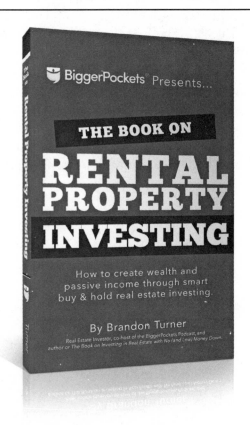

The Book on Rental Property Investing

With nearly 400 pages of in-depth advice and strategies for building wealth through rental properties, *The Book on Rental Property Investing* by BiggerPockets podcast cohost Brandon Turner will teach you how to build an achievable plan, find incredible deals, pay for your rentals, and much more! If you ever thought of using rental properties to build wealth or obtain financial freedom, this book is for you.

If you enjoyed this book, we hope you'll take a moment to check out some of the other great material BiggerPockets offers. BiggerPockets is the real estate investing social network, marketplace, and information hub, designed to help make you a smarter real estate investor through podcasts, books, blog posts, videos, forums, and more. Sign up today—it's free! **Visit www.BiggerPockets.com.**

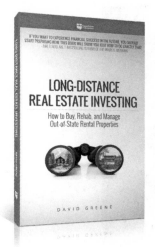

Long-Distance Real Estate Investing

Don't let your location dictate your financial freedom: Live where you want, and invest anywhere it makes sense! The rules, technology, and markets have changed: No longer are you forced to invest only in your backyard. In *Long-Distance Real Estate Investing*, learn an in-depth strategy to build profitable rental portfolios through buying, managing, and flipping out-of-state properties from real estate investor and agent David Greene.

Set for Life: Dominate Life, Money, and the American Dream

Looking for a plan to achieve financial freedom in just five to ten years? *Set for Life* is a detailed fiscal plan targeted at the median-income earner starting with few or no assets. It walks you through three stages of finance, guiding you to your first $25,000 in tangible net worth, then to your first $100,000, and then to financial freedom. *Set for Life* teaches you how to build a lifestyle, career, and investment portfolio capable of letting you live the life of your dreams.

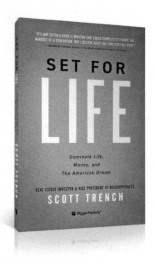

More from
BiggerPockets Publishing

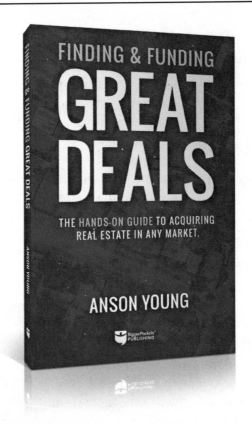

Finding and Funding Great Deals

Learning to find great real estate deals is one of the hardest aspects of becoming a successful investor. In *Finding and Funding Great Deals*, seasoned real estate agent and investor Anson Young guides you through his tried and true methods for finding deals in any market. He outlines his own strategy and walks you through multiple other techniques and tricks to help new and seasoned investors alike improve their real estate business.

The Book on Investing in Real Estate with No (and Low) Money Down

Lack of money holding you back from real estate success? It doesn't have to! In this groundbreaking book from Brandon Turner, author of *The Book on Rental Property Investing*, you'll discover numerous strategies investors can use to buy real estate using other people's money. You'll learn the top strategies that savvy investors are using to buy, rent, flip, or wholesale properties at scale!

The Book on Managing Rental Properties

No matter how great you are at finding good rental property deals, you could lose everything if you don't manage your properties correctly! Change the way you think of being a landlord forever with *The Book on Managing Rental Properties*. Written with both new and experienced landlords in mind, this book takes you on an insider tour of Brandon and Heather Turner's management business so you can discover exactly how they've been able to maximize their profit, minimize their stress, and have a blast doing it!

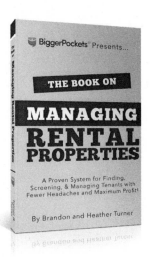

Learn More from BiggerPockets

and Become Successful in Your Real Estate Business Today!

Facebook
/BiggerPockets

Instagram
@BiggerPockets

Twitter
@BiggerPockets

LinkedIn
/company/Bigger
Pockets

Website
BiggerPockets.com